The *Serial* Podcast and Storytelling in the Digital Age

This volume analyzes the *Serial* podcast, situating it in the trajectory of other popular crime narratives and contemporary cultural theory. Contributors focus on topics such as the ethics of the use of fiction techniques in investigative journalism, the epistemological overlay of postmodern indeterminacy, and the audience's prolific activity in social media, examining the competing narrative strategies of the narrators, characters, and audience. Other topics considered include the multiplication of narratives and the longing for closure, how our minds work as we experience true-crime narratives, and what critical race theory can teach us about the program's strategies.

Ellen McCracken is Professor in the Department of Spanish and Portuguese and in the Program in Comparative Literature at the University of California, Santa Barbara, USA.

Routledge Focus on Digital Media and Culture

The *Serial* Podcast and Storytelling in the Digital Age

Edited by Ellen McCracken

LONDON AND NEW YORK

First published 2017 by Routledge

2 Park Square, Milton Park, Abingdon, Oxfordshire OX14 4RN
52 Vanderbilt Avenue, New York, NY 10017

Routledge is an imprint of the Taylor & Francis Group, an informa business

First issued in paperback 2019

Library of Congress Cataloging-in-Publication Data
A catalog record for this book has been requested

ISBN: 978-1-138-62829-8 (hbk)
ISBN: 978-0-367-88717-9 (pbk)

Typeset in Times New Roman
by Apex CoVantage, LLC

Contents

Introduction

The Unending Story

Ellen McCracken

On an ordinary Thursday in October 2014, Chicago public radio WBEZ released a revolutionary new program of investigative journalism. Uploaded to the Internet as an audio podcast, the twelve weekly installments were written and dramatically read by journalist Sarah Koenig. *Serial* caught on like wildfire, fueled by word of mouth and a new mode of participatory interaction with the program on the Internet. Hundreds of thousands of listeners dialogued about the continuing story on Reddit and other social media sites. The audience mushroomed to five million by week six, and a year and a half later it had reached 170 million. No matter that the last episode of Season One aired December 18, 2014—the podcast overflows these temporal boundaries as listeners continue to participate in online discussions, new people engage with the old episodes, updates are released, the news media cover ongoing legal events related to the case, and Season Two introduces another intriguing investigation replete with its own unending narratives. *Serial* created a new kind of intimate storytelling in the digital age. Koenig seems to speak directly and personally to listeners through their earbuds, dramatically reading the carefully crafted text, releasing intriguing information bit-by-bit, and letting them listen in on her private dialogue with the protagonists of the story, whose voices they also hear.

Literature professors became as excited as everyone else about the intriguing new narrative form. In January 2016, the Forum on Popular Culture organized a panel at the Modern Language Association Convention in Austin with four scholarly papers on the new media phenomenon. These presentations became the seeds of this book, and three additional scholars wrote chapters. Analytical tools from narratology, media theory, critical race theory, postmodernism, psychoanalysis, and post-structuralism inform these readings of *Serial*, and the contributors also compare this modern detective story to nineteenth-century precedents and current television shows.

Serial's unconventional melding of certain traditional standards of professional journalism with rule-breaking innovative techniques raised serious questions of ethics that were debated in many articles and forums. Did the reporter become too close to the person she investigated? Did she unabashedly eschew the traditional standards of objectivity taught in journalism schools and revered by both reporters and the public? Was she fair in her investigation, or did a degree of bias shape it? Did the podcast take advantage of the victim and others involved in the case by releasing information that violated their privacy? What new precautions does journalism need to take with the information it releases in the age of unfettered listener response on social media and Web 2.0? Did the perspective of an outsider ethnographer shape the barely addressed issues of racial and ethnic inequality in the story?

Several of the contributions in this volume weigh in on these crucial questions, along with issues of narrative structure, the prolific participation of listeners on social media, and the postmodern epistemology of doubt that overcodes *Serial*. Chapters focus on the modes in which the podcast creates desire in listeners and on the competing narrative strategies of the narrators, characters, and audience. Other topics include the multiplication of narratives and the longing for closure, how our minds work as we experience narratives about real crimes, and what critical race theory can teach us about this podcast's strategies. *Serial* is a historically groundbreaking cultural phenomenon that understandably has attracted the attention of this group of literary scholars, themselves ardent fans of the program.

In Chapter 1, Erica Haugtvedt points to a perhaps unforeseen ethical consequence of *Serial*'s combination of the fictional and the documentary. The tension in *Serial* between telling a story with characters and reporting on events that happen to real people has ethical consequences—the rhetoric of fictionality in the podcast overpowers its news function. Because of the slippage between the real and the fictional and the huge social media participation by listeners on Reddit and other forums, the key prosecution witness in the case suffered painful consequences decades later. Comparing *Serial* to popular nineteenth-century true crime series, Haugtvedt delineates the striking similarities in the narrative strategies of the two genres. Speculation drives both narrative forms forward, as both the detectives and the audiences examine and re-examine evidence. In the nineteenth century, the serial reporting of crime spilled out of its boundaries, bridging fact and fiction in other media such as broadsides, novelizations, dramatizations, and "murder sight-seeing" to crime scenes. In one important nineteenth-century case, forty thousand people attended a criminal's execution, mythifiying him and casting him as gentleman. Is a similar reenvisioning of Syed occurring thanks to the podcast?

Jillian DeMair in Chapter 2 investigates the modes in which *Serial* establishes markers of authenticity to concretize the realness of the story and establish credibility. Why would a journalistic project need to do this, since it is already an account of real events? DeMair argues that, on the contrary, *Serial* is essentially an artistic endeavor and therefore must constantly prove its authenticity. It strives to create credibility and the appearance of reality through its creative narrative strategies. *Serial* constructs an embedded storyworld about a murder and conviction that is simultaneously overlain with a metanarrative about Koenig's reinvestigation and her construction of the embedded story. DeMair expands on theories of audionarratology to demonstrate the ways in which the storyworld constructed in *Serial* depends on elements beyond narration—nonverbal markers such as music, acoustic manipulation, mixing, cutting, and sound effects.

While *Serial* shares the narrative strategies of crime narratives from earlier centuries, it also offers comparisons to contemporary popular crime programs on television. Chapter 3 by David Letzler links narratology and Theory of Mind in analyzing both the telling that occurs in *Serial* and the events told. Pairing two popular crime narratives—an episode of the TV series *Dateline* and Season One of *Serial*—he distinguishes multiple levels of embedded consciousness in the podcast in contrast to the fewer narrative levels of *Dateline*. *Serial* requires much more cognitive work of the audience than *Dateline*. Perhaps to create visceral appeal, the narrator/interviewer of the *Dateline* episode collapses three levels—the interview, the investigation, and the murder—and ventriloquizes an interviewee as she speaks. The *Dateline* narrative offers three embedded states of mind, while the more complicated narrative structure of *Serial* sometimes asks its listeners to read eight states of mind in a single segment, leading to a more profound sense of the characters' interiority. Letzler discusses questions about psychopathy and Theory of Mind and the distinction between cognitive and emotional empathy.

In Chapter 4, Ellen McCracken analyzes the attractive rhetorical tropes of fiction and the overarching code of postmodern indeterminacy that *Serial* employs to draw listeners to Koenig's underlying point of view that Adnan Syed was convicted with inadequate evidence and that Bowe Bergdahl has already been punished enough. Through emplotment, compound focalizations, and dialogism, Koenig creates an outer narrative about an inner narrative of crimes that most listeners do not know the details of. The story does not exist for them until Koenig creates it and encourages them to agree with her point of view. Many of the podcast's listeners, however, engage in negotiated and oppositional strategies of interpretation, interacting in online forums and social media, leaving a material record that in turn is partially integrated into the ongoing episodes. These new forms of audience interaction with audio storytelling in the digital age transform the text into a more lucrative commodity, as a new media star is born, well-paid speaking tours ensue, advertisers flock to buy time on the episodes, and listeners give sponsors their digital footprints by clicking on links.

Departing from Barthes' and Derrida's theorizations of the instability of meaning and the radical plurality of texts, Sandra Kumamoto Stanley in Chapter 5 analyzes the competing narrative strategies that Koenig, Syed, and the audience employ as they jointly attempt to decipher a mystery that will ultimately remain unsolved. Although the audio podcast supplements itself with the written word—documents, diaries, letters, police reports, and call logs—it is unable to fulfill the illusory hope that such written records are monologic narratives with certainty and conclusive findings about guilt or innocence. Instead, postmodern epistemological uncertainty prevails. Syed, for example, refuses to listen to the audio podcast and insists on only reading the transcript, hoping to take the narrative back from the prosecutor through the documentation of the written word. He does not understand, Stanley argues, that linearity, rationality, and verifiability are illusory in writing. Syed most likely hopes that he can anchor a fixed exculpatory narrative from the polysemy of the written transcript. Similarly, listeners employed the written word on many subreddits, debating, documenting, and attempting to attain epistemological certainty about the perpetrator of the crime. Stanley notes that a polyphony of narratives continues to proliferate beyond the twelve episodes in the appeals process, social media discussions, and update episodes released by *Serial*. The public will continue to listen for the next possible narrative resolution, believing in the illusory promise that we will eventually attain knowledge about this crime with certainty.

In Chapter 6, Ryan Engley argues that *Serial* "instantiates its own ethics" through the serial form itself, which pivots on gaps in knowledge, delays, and intervals. In contrast to standard journalism, "truth" in this new form of reporting accrues through hunches, articulated opinions, and the release of tentative, in-process findings. From the optic of Foucault's concept of *parrhesia* (in the sense of "telling all"), Engley argues that the interlocutors Sarah and Adnan risk offending one another with frank speech, engaging in an ethics in which individual subjectivity is not focused internally but linked to others. He brings Lacan to the question of the ethical in *Serial*, arguing that the many gaps that structure *Serial* are the sites in which unconscious desire manifests itself. Engley focuses on the gaps in "truth" and certainty, but one could extend the analysis to the gaps in oral presentation, the spaces of the unsaid in the recorded speech of both the interviewer and the interviewee—from halting diction and fillers to the deliberately censored and unsaid. The continuing process of deferment of the ending, the prospective re-adjudication, and the possibility that more episodes of the first season might be created are essential to listeners' desire, Engley argues. He notes that, seen from the perspective of desire, disappointment is essential to serial storytelling. The ethics of *Serial*, he suggests, is an ethics of desire.

Charli Valdez brings critical race theory to his reading of *Serial* in Chapter 7. He begins with a central question of journalistic ethics: is aestheticizing the tragedy of a real murder justified because the privileged National Public Radio team intervenes in a possible miscarriage of justice? Did the journalist adequately humanize Syed in terms of his Muslim identity, thereby disclosing a reality that the judicial case ignored? Was Koenig also ethically wrong, as some have claimed, by not letting her audience know what she knew and when she knew it? Valdez argues that Koenig engages in "radical transparency," a "self-disclosing ethic" that undercuts the ideology that journalism can ever be objective. Critical race theory would valorize *Serial*'s creation of a counterstory to expose what went untold in the legal case, working its way into the judicial narrative from the outside. However, Valdez argues, ultimately the podcast did not adequately deal with the dimension of race.

Serial's massive popularity across many sectors of the United States and among people engaging with English worldwide is testimony to the power of this new aesthetically enhanced investigative journalism and to the new modes of audience participation that mushroom in the digital age. Kathleen Fitzpatrick has argued that such online participation—specifically personal blogging—helps to construct a new form of subjectivity in which people are not individuals but part of a network. Similarly in *Serial*, the many online discussions of the new cultural phenomenon and the strategies that the podcast employs to make listeners feel they are part of the investigation work to reconfigure individual subjectivity to that of a networked community. Participants in these online discussions thereby inscribe themselves as characters in the narrative of *Serial*—investigators, thinkers, and even new "jury" members, leaving online a public record of this inscription. Further, like *Serial* itself, these online texts are never entirely finished and entice people to check back to read and even participate in the continuing commentary. *Serial* 1 leads to *Serial* 2 and 3, to the updates of Season One released in early February 2016, which we know will lead to further updates as Syed's judicial process continues. Both previous and new audiences listen to the old episodes that now have new ads inserted. We can look forward to movies and TV series about Syed, Lee, and Bergdahl and the subsequent cases *Serial* will investigate.[1] Our relationship to this new cultural text is always in process, enticing us with new developments and opportunities to participate—connected to other participatory members of the huge networked audience.

Note

1. Already, Rabia Chaudry has created a competing podcast, *Undisclosed*, about the case and in August 2016 published a book with her version of the events. Additionally, the TV show *Adnan Syed: Innocent or Guilty?* premiered in June 2016.

Works Cited

Fitzpatrick, Kathleen. "The Pleasure of the Blog: The Early Novel, the Serial, and the Narrative Archive." *Scholarship at Claremont*, 1 Jan. 2007. Web. 12 April 2016.

1 The Ethics of Serialized True Crime

Fictionality in *Serial* Season One

Erica Haugtvedt

On its website, *Serial* claims to tell

> one story—a true story—over the course of a season. Each season, we follow a plot and characters wherever they take us. We won't know what happens at the end until we get there, not long before you get there with us. Each week we bring you the next chapter in the story, so it's important to listen to the episodes in order.
>
> ("About *Serial*")

Serial's audience is thus primed to expect a story with *characters* and a *plot*, for which it is important to listen *in order, serially*. A plot and characters—for true crime? Sarah Koenig doesn't chronicle *characters*; she chronicles *people*—and the tension between these two categories produces one of the ethical dilemmas at the heart of *Serial*.

Starting in October 2014, *Serial* distributed twelve approximately weekly podcasts during its first season. Throughout these episodes, Koenig re-covers the case of Hae Min Lee's murder on January 13, 1999, for which Hae's seventeen-year-old ex-boyfriend, Adnan Syed, was convicted (Koenig "The Alibi"). Adnan's acquaintance, Jay, testified in court that Adnan killed Hae in anger over their breakup; Jay claimed to have helped Adnan bury Hae's body. Witnesses contradict each other, evidence seems to have been missing or overlooked, and Koenig presents the competence of Adnan's defense lawyer as dubious.

The podcast, which is sometimes monotonously pedantic about the details of the years-old case it chronicles, was unexpectedly popular: CNN estimated that the podcast had been downloaded forty million times as of December 23, 2014 (Roberts). As its title suggests, *Serial*'s success is due in no small part to its serial storytelling strategies. The podcast elucidates the capacities of serial form to attract and maintain a dedicated, and even obsessed, audience. The reception of the first season is partially captured in a dedicated discussion forum, called a subreddit, on the website Reddit. Fans speculate on the *Serial* subreddit, sometimes further investigating the leads that Koenig provided. Yet the subreddit runs into trouble when fans discover how easy it is to access the full names and social media accounts of the persons involved in the case. Even as the subreddit, like its host website Reddit, has policy against "doxing"—providing personal information and documents about people who wish to remain private—this policy is difficult to enforce in an online forum regularly flooded with contributions.

When fannish curiosity crosses into violating the privacy of witnesses in the present day, it becomes emphatically clear that *Serial* is dealing *not* with characters but with people whose real lives many years after the crime are invaded by the fandom *Serial* cultivates. *Serial*, therefore, fulfills the potential of its serial narrative form—a form that first realized its potency in the Victorian period, when true crime was serially narrated to similarly obsessive effects. When *This American Life* serialized *Serial*, it did not seem prepared for the consequences. But given the history of serial entertainment, perhaps it should have been.

In the following, I compare *Serial* to serialized true crime in the nineteenth century in order to demonstrate the capacities of serialized narrative to produce an invested and even obsessed audience who plays between fact, speculation, fictionality, and fictionalization. The boundaries between fiction and nonfiction are not absolute, as I will show through how the Elstree murder case of 1823 promiscuously passed between the newspapers, the stage, and the tourist trap. *Serial* unleashes the positive and negative ethical potentialities of serial form. Inspiring a dedicated fandom, *Serial* links episodes to each other through the curiosity of speculation. When the podcast's fans continue that speculation beyond idle chatter online and desire to continue the story by investigating it themselves, then the ethical ramifications of seriality are amplified for the podcast. While *Serial* has the potential to help exonerate a man, the enthusiastic fandom also risks treating the nonfictional as if it were fictional by relating to real people as if they were characters.

History of Serial Form

The media culture that emerged in the late eighteenth century through the nineteenth century saw the proliferation of print entertainment in a variety of forms. Newspapers, periodicals, broadsides, novels in parts, and novels in volume—all of these forms became easier to produce, cheaper, and thus more accessible to a growing population of print consumers throughout the nineteenth century. The century consequently saw the rise of mass entertainment. The masses consumed entertainment voraciously, and the boundaries between news and fiction were porous. Within this context, serial reading unfolded as a practice that fundamentally affected the reception of real and fictional events.

The logic of seriality perpetuates the idea that there is always more to discover, and this impression carries across both nonfictional and fictional uses of serialization. Indeed, the contrast between factual news and fictional entertainment is not so clear-cut. Mark W. Turner explains that the "natural state of being for periodicals is change and movement, and newspapers and periodicals rely, to a greater or lesser degree, on the 'new' and on the very modern concept of advancement, of moving forward, of futurity" (184). News signals change and enforce the sense that audiences must inform themselves regularly in order to stay up to date. News, premised on novelty, is topical, relevant—therefore, definitions of what constitutes news vary widely by publication and intended audience ("News"). While news items like speeches in parliament, natural disasters, or the current price of corn may seem straightforwardly factual, the reporting of sensational murders blurred the line between fact, speculation, and fabrication in ways that reveals the interdependence of journalistic serial narratives and fictional serial narratives.

Scholars of serial narrative have long recognized that serial reading produces a number of specific effects. While William Warner posits that a "pleasure-seeking ethos" is "endemic to serial entertainments" (64), other scholars have suggested that serialization preys upon anxiety in order to drive further consumption. According to Wolfgang Iser, enforced temporal delay leads to deeper imaginative engagement (qtd. in Allen 39). This deeper imaginative engagement allows readers to spend more time speculating and imagining the unresolved story. Rob Allen further suggests that the success of an installment of a serialized narrative is "measured not by readerly satisfaction but readerly desire. The satisfied reader is not sufficient; it is the reader who is insatiable for more that the serial requires" (40). Sean O'Sullivan also finds that satisfaction is "antithetical to the structure and attractions of seriality as a practice," as serial narratives tend to operate *against* containment. In fact, *Serial*'s fans confirm the effect of anxiety and desire when they write of their distress in reaction to Episode 6. Redditor *ctznmatt* writes, "I'm even more confused and distressed than I was last week. And it's not even Thursday yet for me" (Episode 6 Discussion).[1] Redditor *gordanshumway2* agrees: "Distressed is the perfect word" ("Episode 6 Discussion").

Serialization, then, unleashes the considerable power of a desiring, anxious, and invested audience in stories that continually defer closure. This combination is particularly volatile when united with the serial narration of true crime, as the nineteenth century taught us. Victorians routinely sought *more* of horrific crime stories. They read about murders in newspapers and broadsides, they bought serialized novelizations of the crime, and they attended dramatizations. More than this, what historian Judith Flanders has called "murder sight-seeing" was a common pastime (3). Victorians traipsed through crime scenes to look at the dead bodies and steal keepsakes from the scene; they eagerly attended hangings and visited funerals. In 1827, Thomas de Quincey described nineteenth-century audiences: "The world in general . . . are very bloody-minded; and all they want in a murder is a copious effusion of blood" (qtd. in Flanders 19).

The genre of true crime, in the nineteenth century and today, centrally concerns questions of contested guilt, typically in the context of a legal case. Thus, true-crime narratives cultivate audience speculation. This speculation reconfigures the past as participants interrogate degrees of probability regarding the evidence of the case. This interrogation of historical possibilities powerfully resembles participation in fictional worlds in that both depend upon imaginative invention in relation to a constellation of foregoing evidence.[2] The most salient difference is that, while wholly fictional narratives remain fully in the realm of the imaginary, legal interrogation of the past potentially impinges upon the actual world. Legal decisions about what probably happened in the past, regardless of whether it actually happened, have real-world, material consequences for real-world people. True-crime narratives, then, draw upon a common resource with fiction—speculation—but they do so with very different consequences, as true-crime narratives intend to be received as nonfictional. Indeed, it is not always clear that audiences assiduously differentiate between the real and the imaginary—either in the nineteenth century or in the twenty-first.

The nineteenth century powerfully demonstrates that the speculation endemic to true crime does not stay strictly isolated to the rational consideration of evidence; instead, speculation runs over into fictionalized re-tellings and re-imaginings of the crime. The 1823 case of John Thurtell exemplifies traits of serially narrated true crimes in the period: the murder case was the first to have been "tried by newspaper"; Thurtell's crimes were said to have founded newspaper fortunes, and cultural memory of the case would persist into the 1840s (Flanders 20). Fictionalizations like those that derived from Thurtell's case show that, even when the story is true, audiences relate to infamous criminals as characters.

The Elstree Murder

In the first decades of the nineteenth century, John Thurtell had failed as a cloth merchant and lost most of his money gambling (Flanders 22). He defrauded his creditors when he claimed to have been robbed of the money he owed them (Flanders 23). So, Thurtell—deep in debt—encountered William Weare, a notorious and successful gambler who was said to have carried all his savings on his person, rumored to amount to £2,000.

The evidence against Thurtell was fairly clear, and popular opinion during the trial was that he had murdered William Weare. Thurtell conspired with his friends Joseph Hunt and William Probert. On October 24, 1823, Thurtell invited Weare to go hunting in Hertfordshire at Probert's cottage. On the way, Thurtell stopped and shot at Weare; as Thurtell later confessed to his accomplices, the gun misfired, and Thurtell bludgeoned Weare to death with his pistol and then slit his throat (Flanders 25). Thurtell, Hunt, and Probert first buried the body near Probert's cottage but then moved it to a pond farther away.

For any given day during the month after Weare's murder, the four pages of *The Times* consisted of two pages of advertisements, two columns of news, and the rest given over to police, trial, and magistrates' court reports concerning the case (Flanders 27). Newspapers did not feign neutrality. *The Morning Chronicle* called the three men "murderers" before their conviction, and several newspapers printed libelous reports of other supposed murders, rapes, and heinous deeds attributed to Thurtell, Probert, and Hunt. For those who could not afford newspapers, broadsides provided updates on trial reports and included songs and poetic effusions on the subject of the murder, along with illustrations.

Two weeks before the trial was scheduled, fictionalized plays based on the murder were advertised at the Surrey and the Coburg (Flanders 30). A playbill for one of the plays touts sets that are "*illustrated by CORRECT VIEWS taken on the SPOT*" and that have "THE IDENTICAL HORSE AND GIG *Alluded to by the Daily Press*" (Flanders 33–34, emphasis original). This fetishization of the "real" objects of the murder in the play shows how the audience's fascination with what factually happened becomes entangled in fictionalizations that promise to bring the audience experientially closer to the captivating case.

Indeed, Probert's cottage itself became a site of murder tourism where visitors would pay an entrance fee for a tour, which would conclude with purchasing souvenirs—a lucky few were able to buy a bit of the sack in which Weare's body was carried, and others could buy a Staffordshire pottery figure or a book complete with a map of Weare's posthumous journeys (Flanders 35). As late as 1828, Walter Scott wrote that he and his friends paid a woman to give them a tour of the cottage (Flanders 35). Flanders claims that "everything to do with Thurtell had a commercial value" (43).

After Thurtell's conviction, his character as "the drinker of blood" began to disappear in public discourse to be replaced by Thurtell the gallant gentleman (Flanders 40). Such a change reveals how Thurtell was subject to the projected speculations of an audience who knew him only by reputation. It was said that forty thousand people attended Thurtell's execution. One broadside reported that, as Thurtell stood under the scaffold, he looked to the crowd and made a slight bow. In response, every head in the crowd was uncovered, and many murmured "what a gentleman" (Flanders 40). After Thurtell's execution, William Thackeray satirically wrote: "Light be the stones on Thurtell's bones . . . he was the best friend the penny-a-line men had for many a day . . . and when he was turned off, their lamentation was sincere" (Flanders 42). Thomas Carlyle said, "Thurtell being hanged last week, we grew duller than ever" (Flanders 43).

The ways in which Thurtell's case and Thurtell himself were fictionalized and fetishized still occur in the 2014 telling of Adnan Syed's case: namely, the Redditors avidly following the podcast assiduously document its real places and recreate the timelines produced in court, while at the same time interrogating the moral character of witnesses, such as Jay Wilds.

The Rhetoric of Fictionality

The narrative of Thurtell's crimes, investigation, and trial were serially distributed across newspapers and broadsides that reported the news as it unfolded. These numerous reports were more than merely informative; they were entertaining. Soon, Thurtell leaped from the newspapers to the stage, with the real horse and gig used during the crime. Multiple fictionalized versions of the crime testify to the nature of the audience's interest—Thurtell wasn't just a murderer; he was perceived as a *character*, and the serial distribution of his story likely facilitated audiences' sense of intimacy with a criminal whose representation kept reappearing in their lives. Likewise, the interest in *Serial* exceeds any merely informational news function. The producers of *Serial* deliberately shape the narrative to create emotional effects. They craft episodes in order to attract listeners to "tune in next week," and multiple news outlets comment upon the progress of the case and its growing fandom outside the serialization of the podcast proper. *Serial*'s entertainment is facilitated by its serial form, a form that is used in both fictional and nonfictional contexts. Popular crimes like Thurtell's and Syed's reveal how fictionality interpenetrates nonfictional true-crime narration, betraying the degree to which audiences may not assiduously differentiate between how they encounter fiction and nonfiction, even while they are conscious of the differing ontological claims to reality.

Narratologists Henrik Skov Nielsen, James Phelan, and Richard Walsh have recently argued that fictionality is better treated as a rhetoric of communication than as a global mode characteristic of entire texts; they value *communicative intent* as "more significant than any a priori divide between fiction and nonfiction based solely on textual features" (64). Skov Nielsen et al. distinguish between fiction "as a set of conventional genres" and fictionality "as a quality or fictive discourse as a mode" that permeates everyday communication (62).[3] Fictive discourse is distinct from lying since fictive discourse does not try to deceive the audience regarding the actual state of affairs; rather, fictive discourse depends upon "the ability to invent, imagine, and communicate without claims to refer to the actual" (Skov Nielsen et al. 63). Fictionality is invoked when a person invents a hypothetical scenario in order to illuminate or comment upon the real world without explicitly referring to that world in the sense of claiming literal truth; when people use fictional discourse, they do not intend to deceive. Moments of fictional discourse can occur in acts of communication that otherwise have a globally non-fictive intent.

True-crime narratives like *Serial* entertain audiences by comingling discourse that has a global non-fictive intent with moments of fictionality that move away from warranted hypotheses of the case—determined by legal standards of credibility—toward unmoored invention that would not (or perhaps should not) be admissible in a court of law. Even as fans may view their interpretations as supportable, the narrative that will ultimately determine Adnan's fate is decreed by the judicial system. At the same time, *Serial* implicitly invites listeners to treat the podcast like *fictional* crime genres when the podcast claims to tell stories with plot and characters. This slippage between the non-fictive and the fictive, combined with a serial form that has historically facilitated audience immersion, invites *Serial*'s listeners to treat the persons of the case *as if* they were fictional characters. As Skov Nielsen et al. emphasize, "[t]he ability to invent, imagine, and communicate without claim to refer to the actual is a fundamental cognitive skill, one crucial to humans' interactions with their world and their fellow beings in that world" (63). To think in terms of fictionality is to think in terms of hypothesis. Uses of fictionality in non-fictive contexts have a range of positive and negative rhetorical effects, but, in the case of *Serial*, some fans on Reddit sought more of the case by seeking more of its "characters": specifically, Jay. This violation of Jay's privacy raises the question of the ethics of *Serial*'s storytelling strategies. Even as the creators of *Serial* never authorized Jay's harassment by fans, their serial storytelling cultivated the impression of an ongoing investigation in which fans thought they could participate. Thus, the creators of *Serial* are implicated in Jay's harassment even if they are not wholly responsible.

Serial fans probably listen with the assumption that the story is *not* fictive; nonetheless, *Serial*'s serialization and narrative techniques produce a sense of intimacy usually reserved for stories that are our own or are fictional.[4] *Serial* fans treat the remote real-life people of the case as if they were *fictional characters* in the sense that the fans project interiority and motives onto the body and name of a person to whom they do not have personal access. In the *Serial* subreddit, the Redditors talk about "characters" and compare the podcast's genre to *Law and Order* and *CSI*, with little apparent awareness of the generic divide between investigative reporting and fictional crime procedurals ("Episodes 1–2 Discussion").[5] I contend that this happens in part because serial narration serves to resemble both the ongoingness and the futurity of news, while at the same time promoting the expectation of a plotted arc. *Serial* has twelve episodes (in Season One); this awareness pervades the subreddit as fans wonder how Koenig will be able to achieve closure at the end of the season.[6] *Serial*'s resemblance to the episodic fictional crime procedural invites listeners to use the similar generic strategies for interpreting the podcast.[7] Ultimately, the obsessiveness that seriality instantiates instigates the power of a mass audience in ways that *This American Life* seemed unprepared for.

Routes and Reference

Whereas public enthusiasm for Thurtell's case led some people to attend a dramatization where the authentic "HORSE AND GIG" used during the crime were featured, fans of *Serial* seek to further affiliate themselves with the podcast by locating the case's real-world places on Google Maps, researching its real people on social media, and recreating contested timelines of the murder. These moves to "touch" the case through reaching beyond the audio material of the podcast elucidate the fandom's desire to involve themselves in order to feel closer to the story. Koenig participates in this (and may even sanction the impulse) when she and producer Dana Chivvis re-enact the prosecution's timeline of the murder in Episode 5, "Routes." This move to corroboration, seemingly dependent on reference, actually unmoors the theory of the case from historical possibility into the open air of fictional invention.[8]

The prosecution contended that Hae was killed between 2:15 pm and 2:36 pm at the Best Buy parking lot, about a mile from Woodlawn High School. This version of events was premised largely on Jay's testimony. Therefore, corroborating Jay's versions of events becomes a means of testing the probability of the prosecution's case as well as testing the reliability of Jay himself.

"[A twenty-one-minute window to commit the murder] may seem like a long time," Adnan wrote in his first letter to Koenig asking her to take on the project, "but it is virtually impossible if you consider the following facts," which included 1,500 students exiting a four-story school building at once and waiting for school buses to clear the parking lot ("Episode 5

Transcript" 2). Adnan estimated waiting for the buses alone took ten to fifteen minutes. So Koenig and *Serial* producer Chivvis took it upon themselves to test Adnan's claim. They set out to time their movements from every location mentioned—fifteen years after the crime had occurred.

Koenig and Chivvis' task is destined to be an approximation at best and, at worst, to be fantasy. There is no way that they can recover the exact conditions of that January day in 1999.[9] Yet the standard of corroboration enables the illusion of the past's accessibility. Koenig and Chivvis' reenactment solidifies the case's reality for its listeners: this murder may have taken place fifteen years ago, but these settings are not fictional. Their timed trip through Baltimore serves to reinforce audience affiliation in a similar way to the advertised authentic horse and gig in the dramatization of Thurtell's crime.

Although Adnan had hoped that any reenactment of the twenty-one-minute timeline would clearly reveal its impossibility, Koenig and Chivvis were able to mostly corroborate the prosecution's timeline. "[W]e were like a machine," Koenig says ("Episode 5 Transcript" 3). The bus loop does in fact take a few minutes to clear, but Koenig and Chivvis are nonetheless able to park at the alleged spot where the murder took place at Best Buy—which is still there today—in eighteen minutes ("Episode 5 Transcript" 6). They calculate 1.5 minutes for manual strangulation ("Episode 5 Transcript" 8). Then, they walk over to where the payphone supposedly was at Best Buy and place the 2:36 pm call during which Adnan allegedly asked Jay to come pick him up ("Episode 5 Transcript" 6). In total, Koenig and Chivvis reenacted the timeline from after school until Hae's murder in twenty-two and a half minutes.

Chivvis and Koenig pause to consider the probability of the prosecution's theory: "I mean, it seems like, yeah it could be done. But it seems far fetched," Chivvis surmises ("Episode 5 Transcript" 8). Koenig agrees:

> there's no room for any errors. Any pauses even. The buses, the drive, the strangulation. The moving of the body. The call. They all have to happen as quickly as they possibly can for the 2:36 call to work. But, it is possible. Or at least not impossible.
>
> ("Episode 5 Transcript" 8)

The timeline is possible; it is not highly *probable*, because they were so machine-like, leaving the least amount of possible time between scheduled tasks. They are unable to disprove the timeline's possibility but still entertain significant doubts about its probability.

Yet Jay's version of events seemed convincing to the jury. At trial, the prosecution displayed a big chart of the call record listing the thirty-four calls made and received on Adnan's cell phone that day, with blanks beside each call ("Episode 5 Transcript" 10). Every time a witness identified a call made on that list, the prosecution would label the call with a sticker ("Episode 5 Transcript" 10). Adnan says, "It was a pretty powerful thing. Because as [Jay] was testifying, it was almost as if they were using the cell phone records as proof for all the testimony" ("Episode 5 Transcript" 10). Indeed, in her closing argument, prosecutor Casey Murphy said,

> The most important thing for you to remember about Jay's testimony is that it does not stand alone. It is corroborated. . . . The cell phone records support what those witnesses say, and the witnesses support what those cell phone records say.
>
> ("Episode 5 Transcript" 10)

The cell phone record, more than Jay himself, is the most powerful witness in the case—the pings to cell phone towers throughout Baltimore testify to the probability of Adnan's cell phone's location, implicating him and Jay in the murder and burial of Hae Min Lee.[10] History seems accessible and recoverable. The prosecution offers a theory of the crime that fits neatly with historical evidence.

Even as Koenig and Chivvis were unable to *disprove* the 1999 timeline up until 2:36 pm, the prosecution's timeline after that point increasingly unraveled—especially the version in which Jay and Adnan head to Patapsco State Park to smoke marijuana before Adnan's track practice at 4 pm. Throughout the episode, the timeline increasingly looks more like an act of invention. "It's like . . . *Trying to plot the coordinates of someone's dream,*" Koenig says ("Episode 5 Transcript" 16, emphasis added). She's more right than perhaps she knows. The effort to recreate the timed experience of the crime elucidates the degree to which Jay's story cannot be referentially corroborated and therefore highlights the emergent fictionality of this episode's narrative. Even the version of events ultimately privileged in court is selective and blind to existing facts. As Koenig and Chivvis drive around Baltimore, they realize that there are multiple versions of events, none of which cohere into a clear version of the truth. Instead, Koenig and Chivvis' attempt to recover the past only dramatizes the degree to which that recovery is impossible. They have only fragments and *versions* of events, not a reliable history.[11]

All of these questions of corroboration and reliability circle back to Jay. Throughout his multiple slightly conflicting versions of the day, Jay seems to be purposefully misleading the police. Yet when Adnan's defense lawyer, Cristina Gutierrez, accused Jay of lying on the stand, Jay insists, "No, I told [the police] the truth," after having just admitted that his statements "were not the truth" moments earlier ("Episode 5 Transcript" 28). "They weren't the truth. What is the opposite of the truth?" Gutierrez presses. Jay responds: "I told them the truth, I did not show them a location that was true, no" ("Episode 5 Transcript" 29). Gutierrez wants to establish that the opposite of the truth is lying. But there is a space between truth and lies that lets Jay claim that he is telling the truth even as he is misleading according to particular facts, and that space belongs to the truth of fictionality. Koenig channels this when she interprets Jay's stance: "Yes, I told some lies, but I told the truth. Overall, I told the truth" ("Episode 5 Transcript" 29).

The Ethics of the Telling and the Fandom

If Episode 5 revealed how Jay's statements do not cohere, the podcast's methods of telling invite the audience to identify with Koenig and Chivvis as investigators and, implicitly, to continue to question missing pieces in this story. Koenig and Chivvis sound friendly, chatty, and approachable. "There's a shrimp sale at the Crab Crib," Chivvis chirps during Episode 5, which prompts Koenig to confide, "Sometimes I think Dana isn't listening to me" ("Episode 5 Transcript" 14). The subreddit participants typically refer to Koenig as "Sarah," demonstrating a degree of assumed familiarity that may not be equally true of other journalists who narrate true crime ("Episode 5 Discussion").[12] Koenig's chattiness cultivates an entertaining listening experience, especially in a podcast that risks getting bogged down in the workings of cell phone towers. Yet, at the same time, her ethos invites the audience to think that they too could investigate the case—and, indeed, they do.

The serialized format of the podcast both cultivates anxiety and desire for more of the story *and* gives fans the time to investigate the leads Koenig has provided before the next episode. Indeed, the subreddit discussions both meticulously pull apart the latest podcast episode and speculate about what will happen next in the podcast, and what could have actually happened back in 1999. After Episode 5, Redditor *hardly_descartes* writes, "It seems the most important thing we learned from this episode . . . is that *none* of the versions of Jay's stories of what happened that day are compatible with the cell phone data" ("Episode 5 Discussion"). Redditor *cupcake310* writes, "I can't help but to think that there are so many inconsistencies because both Jay and Adnan are lying," to which *glamorousglue* replies, "They both downplay their relationships to one another, don't they?" ("Episode 5 Discussion"). Speculation that occurs within the confines of the content of the podcast soon moves toward speculation based on information obtained outside of the podcast. Redditor *jellysleuth* writes that although Adnan's family friend Rabia had recently redacted the cell phone logs from her public blog, "Luckily I had saved them before the redaction, so now know the full names of the people contacted that afternoon" ("Episode 5 Discussion"). Given the age of the case, locating public records with the full names of the people involved is easy; indeed, Redditors follow the public Facebook profile of Jay as long as it is available. The subreddit has entire threads titled "The case for and against Don" and "Speculation: My thoughts on who else might have been involved" (*Serial* subreddit). The activity of speculating beyond the boundaries of what the podcast strictly states is clearly central to the subreddit.

Yet the *Serial* subreddit displays its policy against doxing in a column that appears on the right-hand side of the landing page: "Do not share or request personal information that was not included in the podcast or other official source" (*Serial* subreddit). The subreddit's policy mirrors the policy of Reddit as a whole. Reddit discourages doxing for good reason—speculation led to public vigilantism that has gotten the website into trouble before.

Following the Boston Marathon bombings on April 15, 2013, Redditors took it upon themselves to identify the bomber. By pooling their labor, Redditors soon pinpointed the missing Brown University student Sunil Tripathi as one of the Boston Marathon bombers by poring over photographs of the crowd. Journalists watching the forum picked up the crowdsourced rumor and retweeted it, effectively legitimizing Reddit's speculation. But Reddit was wrong. The missing student was later discovered to have died, and Tripathi's family was devastated by the smearing of Tripathi's reputation.

Following the public aftermath of Reddit's well-intentioned but ultimately disastrous citizen investigation, Tripathi's sister observed that the space between social media and law enforcement is "porous" (Oremus). While Tripathi's family had hoped that speculation, like that on Reddit, would have been enclosed within social media space, Tripathi's case demonstrates that the space of journalism and the space of social media are open to each other. *Slate Magazine*'s Will Oremus and other media pundits credit this porousness to the advent of new media, when speculation is "broadcast on Twitter one moment, amplified on Twitter the next, and . . . essentially become[s] national news before a single reporter has picked up the phone." But what Oremus is describing is the amplification of *seriality*, and, as we have seen, Thurtell's 1823 case reveals that the porousness between speculation and fact is endemic to serialized media itself; there is nothing fundamentally new about it.

Reddit moderators assiduously take down any information that violates the policy against doxing (Wade). Yet the *Serial* subreddit is huge—it had 50,643 participants as of March 2016—and moderators can seldom keep up. Julie Snyder, a producer for *Serial*, has commented on the investigative activities of the *Serial* subreddit:

> I love the discussions on the site and think it's really incredible listeners are engaging with this story but, yeah, I have to admit I feel a pit in my stomach at the thought of anyone "outing" real people or contacting them or anything like that.
>
> (Dean)

Serial never explicitly tells people to go out and investigate the case themselves, yet Koenig implies, by drawing upon the generic tropes of fictional crime procedurals and the openness of seriality, that the audience can intervene in this ongoing problem. And when the fans *do* try to figure out the case, it seems disingenuous to not admit that this reaction is a consequence of the storytelling choices the podcast has made.

Still, I understand the vertigo Snyder alludes to when she considers fans "outing" real people—because the ethical ramifications are real and sobering. Even though there are also potential *positive* ethical outcomes to the investigation of Adnan Syed's case, *negative* ethical outcomes have already occurred: Jay.

Although Jay is never formally interviewed for the podcast by Koenig herself, he agreed to be interviewed by Natasha Vargas-Cooper for a three-part series of articles in *The Intercept* in December 2014. There, Jay says that he "feels strongly that he was unfairly depicted by Koenig and that she painted a highly misleading portrayal of him and his role in the case" (Vargas-Cooper, part 1). Jay implies that Koenig's investigation is equivalent to "harassing," and he points out the pain for many people in going back and "revisit[ing] this crap" (Vargas-Cooper, part 2). From Jay's perspective, the case is closed, and he insists that the only person for whom he would answer unanswered questions would be Hae's mom (Vargas-Cooper, part 2). Nonetheless, Jay is thrust into the spotlight against his will.

"The thing that's been the most scary for my family has been people showing up at my house. Twice I've caught people videotaping our home and me," Jay tells Vargas-Cooper (part 3). Jay's home address has been posted in the subreddit, and Jay now worries for the safety of his family (Vargas-Cooper, part 3). Even though moderators eventually delete doxing posts, "sometimes stuff would be left on Reddit about me for days and weeks at a time," Jay says (Vargas-Cooper, part 3). Jay blames the podcast for the loss of his employment; he was laid off after his name started to become associated with murder (Vargas-Cooper, part 3). Ultimately, Jay claims, "[Koenig] created an evil archetype of me and sensationalized my motives. It helped fan the flames of this story that people had already moved on from" (Vargas-Cooper, part 3). Jay recognizes that he has become *Serial*'s villain.

The *Serial* podcast renders Jay a character in a story. Redditor *bast007* observed in the discussion of Episodes 1–2:

> "If [Adnan] is innocent, then Jay would HAVE to be the murderer," to which *bnarows* replies "My wife and I like to watch law and order reruns and this seems to be one of the commonly used beginnings to a show."
>
> ("Episode 1 & Episode 2 Discussion")

Redditor *bast007*'s logic is the logic of fiction: given the way that *Serial* has told the story, Jay would likely be the murderer. Redditor *bnarows* seems to sanction that logic when he transfers generic expectations from *Law & Order* to *Serial*. But *Serial* is not fiction, and Jay is not the inevitable villain.

Although serialization works to integrate the story into the lives of its fans, Adnan Syed's case is at once historically remote and immediately relevant to Jay in a way that it can never be for the rest of us. Fan communities, like that on the *Serial* subreddit, do stoke the fires of serial narratives in the spaces between episodes—spaces that cultivate desire and distress as fans hunger for more information. Reddit's crowdsourced investigations may achieve breakthroughs, but they risk maligning the reputations of people who are no longer on trial. These ambivalent ethical consequences are the fruits of *Serial*'s serial form and its invocation of fictionality in trying to corroborate a version of the past by "plotting the coordinates of a dream." *Serial* may help achieve the exoneration of Adnan Syed. But, in the meantime, the slippage between the real and the fictional has already had consequences for Jay, a man who is not a fictional character and who has not been found guilty of this crime.

Notes

1. All Reddit usernames are italicized.
2. Wolfgang Iser writes, "It is the process of anticipation and retrospection that forms the virtual dimension, which in turn transforms the text into an experience for the reader. Thus, the reality of the reading experience can illuminate basic patterns of real experience" (281).
3. Skov Nielsen et al.'s thesis on the rhetoric of fictionality opposes approaches such as Dorrit Cohn's that see fiction as distinctive. Cohn defines fiction as "literary nonreferential narrative text," and she opposes the conceptual shading of fiction into other meanings, including fiction as untruth, fiction as conceptual abstraction, fiction as all literature, and fiction as all narrative (1–2). I agree that all narratives are not necessarily fiction, but I distinguish between narratives that attempt to recreate historically corroborated "truth" and narratives that

momentarily unmoor themselves through hypothetical speculation that meets Skov Nielsen et al.'s definition of fictionality.

4. See Catherine Gallagher's argument for the rise of fictional Nobodies in *Nobody's Story*, and Alan Palmer's discussion of the apparent intimacy that omniscient narration affords for fictional characters in *Social Minds*.

5. In terms of slipping between characters and people, Redditor *SerialFan* writes, "the girl who was in the library (I really need to make a character list because I keep forgetting names)" ("Episode 1 & Episode 2 Discussion"). Redditor *Royalat136* quotes extensively from John Houseman describing the *War of the Worlds* radio play: "we had to slide swiftly and imperceptibly out of the 'real' time of a news report into the 'dramatic' time of a fictional broadcast" ("Episode 1 & Episode 2 Discussion"). Redditor *rhnoxv10* writes, "Might sound pretty silly—but from whatever little knowledge I have about murders from watching CSI—time of death is usually calculated by body temperature" ("Episode 1 & Episode 2 Discussion"). Redditors are thus using their knowledge of fictional genres to inform their reception of *Serial*, while *Royalat136* seems to be suggesting that the podcast is purposefully exploiting the slippage between nonfiction and fiction.

6. Redditor *nickbfromct* writes, "I hate thinking (knowing) that even by the end of this podcast we still won't know the truth because it's not like Adnan or anyone is going to all of a sudden confess" ("Episode 4 Discussion").

7. Importantly, fictional crime procedurals privilege closure at the end of each episode, whereas a serial narrative typically defers or resists complete closure at the end of each episode and might achieve closure at the end of a season.

8. *Serial* depends on speculation, an activity proximate to but not the same as fictive invention. Speculation is inherent in all legal cases and is distinct from fictionality in that legal theories are subject to real-world reference and responsible to evidence. As Dorrit Cohn argues, this additional level of historical referentiality adds to the story/discourse model of fiction and potentially differentiates nonfictional from fictional communication (112). Cohn argues for fiction's distinctiveness and therefore opposes approaches like Skov Nielsen, Phelan, and Walsh's that understand fictionality as pervading nonfictional contexts. *Serial* intends to be received as nonfiction, and Koenig strives to uphold journalistic integrity by rigorously documenting the evidence of the case and limiting her theories of the crime to those supported by that evidence. Nonetheless, the reenactment of the prosecution's timeline of the murder dramatizes the degree to which theories can be more or less probable considering the evidence, and it raises the specter of speculative invention in historical narrativization. As I will show, explanations of the past become more and more fictionalized as they become unmoored from possible corroboration.

9. Redditors *nadirhotel* and *thesaifking* raise this issue on the *Serial* podcast subreddit when *nadirhotel* asks if there had been any roads created or lanes added in the area since 1999 that would make it quicker to get around in a twenty-minute window; *thesaifking* adds the question of construction in the school that might have made it easier/harder to get out of, and also considers whether the parking lot is set up in the same way ("Episode 5 Discussion").

10. The phone records present their own challenges. Koenig has been unable to confirm the existence of a payphone at Best Buy in 1999 ("Episode 5 Transcript" 6). The usage of cell phone data may have been more unreliable than the court knew at the time—cell phone data is now inadmissible in Oregon and Illinois ("Episode 5 Transcript" 20).

11. My mapping of Koenig and Chivvis' reenactment of the prosecution's timeline is premised upon an understanding of narrative as a possible world. For more on this approach to narrative, see Marie-Laure Ryan, *Narrative as Virtual Reality* (2003). See also work by Hilary Dannenberg, Thomas Pavel, and Ruth Ronen.
12. In the "Episode 5 Discussion" subreddit, for example, *unetortue* and *nadirhotel* both refer to Koenig as Sarah. More instances occur, but I have not exhaustively counted them in all the discussions.

Works Cited

"About *Serial*." *Serial* website. *WBEZ Chicago*. Web. 5 Jan. 2016.

Allen, Rob. "Pause You Who Read This: Disruption and the Victorian *Serial* Novel." In *Serialization in Popular Culture*. Ed. Rob Allen and Thijs van den Berg. New York: Routledge, 2014. Print. 33–46.

Cohn, Dorrit. *The Distinction of Fiction*. Baltimore: Johns Hopkins University Press, 1999. Print.

Dannenberg, Hilary. *Coincidence and Counterfactuality: Plotting Time and Space in Narrative Fiction*. Lincoln: University of Nebraska Press, 2008. Print.

Dean, Michelle. "Listeners of Podcast Phenomenon Turn Detectives: With Troubling Results." *The Guardian*. 7 Nov. 2014. Web. 8 Mar. 2016.

Flanders, Judith. *The Invention of Murder: How the Victorians Revelled in Death and Detection and Created Modern Crime*. New York: St. Martin's, 2011. Print.

"Episode 1 & Episode 2 Discussion." *Episode Guide, Transcripts, and Discussion*. Reddit.com/r/serialpodcast. Web. 5 Jan. 2016.

"Episode 3 Discussion." *Episode Guide, Transcripts, and Discussion*. Reddit.com/r/serialpodcast. Web. 7 Mar. 2016.

"Episode 4 Discussion." *Episode Guide, Transcripts, and Discussion*. Reddit.com/r/serialpodcast. Web. 7 Mar. 2016.

"Episode 5 Discussion." *Episode Guide, Transcripts, and Discussion*. Reddit.com/r/serialpodcast. Web. 7 Mar. 2016.

"Episode 5 Transcript." *Episode Guide, Transcripts, and Discussion*. Reddit.com/r/serialpodcast. Web. 7 Mar. 2016.

"Episode 6 Discussion." *Episode Guide, Transcripts, and Discussion*. Reddit.com/r/serialpodcast. Web. 7 Mar. 2016.

Gallagher, Catherine. *Nobody's Story: The Vanishing Acts of Women Writers in the Marketplace, 1670–1920*. Berkeley: University of California Press, 1995. Print.

Iser, Wolfgang. *The Implied Reader: Patterns of Communication in Prose Fiction from Bunyan to Beckett*. Baltimore: Johns Hopkins University Press, 1974. Print.

"News." In *Dictionary of Nineteenth-Century Journalism*. Ed. Laurel Brake and Marysa Demoor. Gent: Academia Press, 2009: 448. Print.

Oremus, Will. "Don't Blame Reddit for Smearing Sunil Tripathi. Blame 'Retweets Aren't Endorsements.'" *Slate Magazine*. 26 July 2013. Web. 7 Mar. 2016.

O'Sullivan, Sean. "*Serials* and Satisfaction." *Romanticism and Victorianism on the Net. Erudit*. 63 (Apr. 2013). Web. 5 Jan. 2016.

Palmer, Alan. *Social Minds in the Novel*. Columbus, OH: Ohio State University Press, 2010. Print.

Pavel, Thomas. *Fictional Worlds*. Cambridge, MA: Harvard University Press, 1989. Print.

Roberts, Amy. "The '*Serial*' Podcast: By the Numbers." *CNN*. 23 Dec. 2014. Web. 17 Sept. 2016.

Ronen, Ruth. *Possible Worlds in Literary Theory*. Cambridge: Cambridge University Press, 1994. Print.

Ryan, Marie-Laure. *Narrative as Virtual Reality: Immersion and Interactivity in Literature and Electronic Media*. Baltimore: Johns Hopkins University Press, 2003. Print.

Skov Nielsen, Henrik, Jim Phelan and Richard Walsh. "Ten Theses bout Fictionality." *Narrative* 23.1 (Jan. 2015): 61–73. Print.

Turner, Mark W. "Periodical Time in the Nineteenth-Century." *Media History* 8.2 (2002): 183–196. Print.

Vargas-Cooper, Natasha. "Exclusive: Jay, Key Witness From '*Serial*,' Tells His Story for First Time, Part 1." *The Intercept*. 29 Dec. 2014. Web. 7 Mar. 2016.

———. "Jay Speaks Part 2: 'Hae Was Dead Before She Got to My House. Anything that Makes Adnan Innocent Doesn't Involve Me." *The Intercept*. 30 Dec. 2014. Web. 7 Mar. 2016.

———. "Jay Speaks Part 3: The Collateral Damage of an Extremely Popular Podcast about Murder." *The Intercept*. 31 Dec. 2014. Web. 5 Jan. 2016.

Wade, Chris. "The Reddit Reckoning." *Slate Magazine*. 15 Apr. 2014. Web. 5 Jan. 2016.

Warner, William. *Licensing Entertainment: The Elevation of Novel Reading in Britain, 1684–1750*. Berkeley: University of California Press, 1998. Print.

2 Sounds Authentic

The Acoustic Construction of *Serial*'s Storyworld

Jillian DeMair

Crime fiction is often more about the process of detection than the crime itself, and the same is true of the podcast *Serial*. According to Tzvetan Todorov's structural analysis, detective fiction is concerned with two stories: "the story of the crime and the story of the investigation" (44). The first season of *Serial*, produced and narrated by Sarah Koenig, is characterized by precisely the same duality that Todorov locates in detective novels. At the forefront of *Serial* is the story of Hae Min Lee's murder and of what her friends and acquaintances, especially Adnan Syed, were doing on January 13, 1999, and in the days leading up to the murder. The second story is the detailed account of Sarah Koenig's efforts to uncover the truth about the first story. This story is secondary, but Koenig's role as detective is nonetheless an essential part of the podcast and likely has a good deal to do with its popularity. My claim that *Serial* consists of two stories is central to my larger argument that Koenig uses techniques that draw on narrative conventions more frequently seen in fiction that engage listeners and encourage them to suspend their disbelief. I do not intend to suggest fictionality by using terms such as "story" and "narrative." Instead, I am borrowing the term "storyworld" from narratology to refer to the characters, setting, physical laws, social rules, and events that make up the world of either fiction or nonfiction (Ryan and Thon 35–36). Even if a podcast depicts events that actually happened, we are immersed in a carefully crafted storyworld all the same. Similarly, I follow Dorrit Cohn as recognizing "narrative" as an attribute of both literary and historical writing. Cohn, following Paul Ricoeur and others, argues against identifying fiction with narrative; instead, fiction is specifically "nonreferential narrative" (9). In the case of nonfiction such as *Serial*, the real world is our referent, and the listener must decide to what degree the storyworld corresponds to it.

In discussing *Serial* as a meticulously constructed narrative, I consider some of the subtle, often nonlinguistic audio cues that sustain this captivating story. I argue that the first season of *Serial*, which is overtly engaged in finding out the truth about a crime, is also more subtly occupied with signaling the authenticity and legitimacy of the story that is reported. And yet we know that this is a true story about real people, many of whom continue to be affected by the crime. Why would *Serial*'s producers need to emphasize how real the story is? It will become clear that the same storytelling conventions are used to establish credibility in both fictional and nonfictional narratives. *Serial* uses "reality effects," to borrow Roland Barthes' term, which we otherwise often see in fiction, to signify "concrete reality" ("Reality" 146). For example, Sarah Koenig's presentation of archival material mimics the literary convention often called a "discovered manuscript fiction," in which a narrator claims to have received information from a credible source, compiled the facts from a historical chronicle, or acquired some artifact that authenticates the claim. These claims are not necessarily false, but they are a common framing device for realist novels (Bracher 62). The apparent divide between the two parts of my argument—that *Serial* relies on real-life authentication and also on crime fiction conventions—disappears when one considers that narrative so often relies on authenticating effects and a guise of reality to tell a good story, regardless of the story's degree of correlation with historical events.

Serial's Storyworld

Each episode of *Serial* is a compilation of previously recorded conversations, interrogations, and other audio clips, all crafted into a coherent narrative by a host, Sarah Koenig, who presents these recordings and speaks directly to the audience about her efforts to get to the bottom of the 1999 murder. The podcast is also self-consciously occupied with the problems of authentic storytelling. Koenig constantly tries to get to the "truth" behind conflicting stories by comparing them with other evidence and discussing the probability that someone is lying or simply not remembering correctly. At the same time, she reminds us of the facts she has already revealed, or she suggests there is more to come, thereby lending credibility to her own reportage. But can we really say that *Serial* creates its own storyworld as opposed to just talking about stories? Bruce Jackson helpfully explores the distinction: "If I were to say, 'This is a story about a man named Fred who took a wrong turn on a country road and found true love,' I wouldn't be telling a story; I'd be talking about one" (9). So when does the talking about stories end and the telling begin? Does *Serial* actually tell a story? Koenig certainly talks a lot about stories: Adnan Syed's story, Jay's story, Asia's story, Hae Min Lee's story according to her diary. Koenig talks about the difficulties in obtaining the stories and the inconsistencies between them. One could even claim that her documentary and journalistic approach does not comprise a narrative but rather comprises an assortment of data and evidence. But this would mean ignoring the detail dedicated to Koenig's investigation, which becomes a story in its own right. I argue, therefore, that *Serial* is a narrative endeavor, that it is essentially storytelling and can be analyzed as such. As a storyteller, Koenig reflects a great deal on the conditions of the story's production and on the kinds of meaning produced by different sources. The final product itself is the story of how Koenig investigated a number of other stories, and nested within that frame are the stories that tell us about the murder.

In order to examine Koenig's podcast more closely as a narrative endeavor, I use some of the tools established by the field of narratology. A relatively recent development in this field is media-conscious or transmedial narratology, as explored in Marie-Laure Ryan and Jan-Noël Thon's 2014 volume, *Storyworlds across Media*. This branch of narratology, which includes audionarratology, considers the different manifestations of storyworlds across media and expands the understanding of narrative beyond a traditional conception of narrative as language based (2–3). In doing so, media-conscious narratology builds on David Herman's conception of "postclassical narratology." Beginning in 1997, Herman expanded the study of storytelling beyond structuralist models to a more cognitive approach—focusing on the concept of scripts in particular—to account for the perceived narrativity of any given sequence (1053). Media-conscious narratology considers narrativity through an examination of such nonlinguistic phenomena as gestures (Cassell and McNeill 134), pictorial narrativity, and musical narrativity, as well as paraverbal elements such as intonation and tone (Huwiler, *Erzähl-Ströme* 59; Schmedes 74). This approach provides a way of examining narrative in radio plays, graphic novels, film, video games, and other media (Ryan, Introduction 9). Studying *Serial* with these theories allows us to see the ways in which narrative forms are not necessarily "literary or word-oriented" and to perceive that language need not be privileged over other narrative elements—in this case, acoustic ones (Huwiler, "Storytelling" 46). *Serial*, for example, goes well beyond the act of telling through its use of pauses, music, and sound effects, all of which contribute to the overall mental image built by the interpreter. As Ryan explains in an earlier investigation of media and narrative, *Narrative across Media* (2004), narrative is anchored both as an act of representation and as a mental image (Introduction 9). The first entails language as the "native tongue of narrative," but, in cognitive terms, a good deal more can contribute to our interpretation (Introduction 11). We can understand how the overall storyworld is dependent on elements beyond narration if we consider how much our interpretation of *Serial* would differ if we were to read a transcript of Koenig's episodes rather than listen to them. How, then, can we study the nonverbal manifestations of narrative? While podcasts have been less studied, radio has been, and the insights of Elke Huwiler, who offers a narratological model for the analysis of radio plays, are particularly helpful to the present endeavor. I will consider how the technical features that Huwiler highlights—such as acoustic manipulation, mixing, cutting, sound effects, and pauses—shape *Serial* listeners' understanding of what is being told. In addition, the powerful music of *Serial* deserves mention, as it conveys various meanings throughout each episode, such as anticipation, alienation, or apprehension (Huwiler, *Erzähl-Ströme* 61).

Nonverbal Acoustic Storytelling

Huwiler's approach to German radio plays is related to the basic tenets of media-conscious narratology insofar as Huwiler moves beyond forms of analysis that see radio plays primarily as a literary genre and that privilege language over other acoustic elements. Apart from recent developments in "audionarratology," studies that challenge the preeminence of the spoken word in radio drama and other auditory media remain sparse.[1] Huwiler's approach can help us think more deeply about *Serial*, especially insofar as she keeps the unique possibilities of "non-verbal acoustical elements" of storytelling at the forefront of her work ("Storytelling" 50). Sharing a common basis with media-conscious or transmedial narratology, Huwiler starts from Herman's conception of postclassical narratology and moves to a consideration of how technical features such as acoustical manipulation, mixing, and cutting shape the audience's understanding ("Storytelling" 51). The human voice can also be used to convey meaning beyond linguistic content through such aspects as intonation and tone. Huwiler, following Götz Schmedes in his 2002 book on the semiotics of radio drama, categorizes these as "paraverbal" codes (*Erzähl-Ströme* 59; Schmedes 74). Of particular interest to Huwiler and also to my interpretation of *Serial* are the paraverbal and other acoustic devices that are medium specific. As Huwiler argues, acoustic storytelling need not be seen as "merely another medium of literary or dramatic expression" ("Storytelling" 57). Instead, the potential of this particular storytelling form allows for a unique kind of interpretation.

One of the techniques that Koenig uses in the first episode and throughout the season is the insertion of audio clips from previously recorded situations. The reference to seemingly unscripted audio serves as an authenticating device. Due to the interruption in the narrative, the listener is encouraged to forget Koenig as the storyteller for a moment and to hear for themselves "how it really was."[2] The change in audio quality as well as the unscripted aspect of these moments set a different tone for the listener, contributing—I would argue—to a momentary deeper engagement, as when a reader or listener becomes absorbed in the embedded tale of a literary frame narrative and forgets the outermost frame. Koenig employs this device frequently throughout all of the episodes, but not all embedded sound recordings are alike. I follow Huwiler in differentiating between two primary types of archival audio. Some are interviews conducted specifically for *Serial*'s production, while others belong to the category of what Huwiler calls "Originalton" ("original sound bite" or "direct quote" [*Erzähl-Ströme* 67]). An example of the former would be when we hear clips of Koenig's telephone conversations with Adnan Syed and her interviews with other relevant parties, while examples of "Originalton" include archival audio from Syed's trial and police interview tapes.

We hear the first example of audio created specifically for the podcast around the two-minute mark of the first episode of *Serial*. Interestingly, the audio clip is not related in any way to Syed's trial but consists instead of a few clips of interviews Koenig conducted with teenagers in order to demonstrate the difficulty of remembering the events of a specific day six weeks prior, a situation analogous to the case in question ("The Alibi," *Serial* 1.1, 3 October 2014, 2:09–2:26). These exchanges that Koenig has with teenagers who are not involved in the case play an important role in establishing authenticity. These teenagers have nothing to do with the case, and the listener is meant to think that there is no reason they would be anything but their authentic selves. We do not know the identity of the first boy we hear speaking, but his tone and the laughter of his friends in the background reveal that the conversation takes place in a casual setting. The setting together with his use of African American Vernacular English give listeners two important hints: first, that conversations Koenig replays are highly unscripted and that a sense of naturalness and openness underlies them, and, second, that she, a white producer, is not hesitant to engage with members of a minority community, which will become necessary in her investigation of this Baltimore murder case. This audio clip thereby subtly wins the trust of the listener with auditory cues that are purely paraverbal.

Another technique the producers of *Serial* use when inserting prerecorded material, whether created for the podcast or from court files, is sound mixing. Koenig often begins to interject commentary on top of the audio feed that is playing in order to explain or summarize its contents to the listener. Sometimes the original audio fades out at this point, but at other times it continues at low volume beneath Koenig's narrative and then resumes at regular volume when Koenig stops speaking. This happens, for example, with one of the taped police interviews with Jay that Koenig presents in the first episode. Unlike with longer prerecorded clips, where the listener is temporarily immersed in an embedded storyworld, this technique of mixing retains the listener's awareness of the secondary, outer storyworld (the storyworld of Koenig's investigation), while, at the same time, Koenig's authoritative voice dominates our impression of it. These moments, unlike the many where Koenig's voice is the only audio we hear, have a polished quality to them that subtly convinces us of Koenig's authority as a storyteller who has received her information firsthand. The use of her voice to summarize others' stories is particularly convincing when the original sources of those other stories remain audibly present, in contrast to the sections in which we hear only her voice reflecting on the investigative process. An example of this mixing with voice-over can be found in her use of the taped police interviews with Jay in the first episode. We hear clips of the police interview, and then Koenig's explanations, while the audio continues to run quietly in the background. Since the audio continues under Koenig's explanations, we know we have missed part of the original, but we probably barely wonder about it since we have the narrator's voice providing context and synopsis. Both Huwiler and Schmedes identify three main types of technical modifications that contribute to the continuity of a radio play: fading, cutting, and mixing. Although the two audio tracks run concurrently in this example from *Serial*, this is in fact an example of fading, since the police interview audio fades to a lower volume when Koenig's audio is inserted and Koenig's audio does not continue throughout. *Serial* employs this technique frequently. When used in the radio drama, the technique of fading signifies a relationship—of connection or distance—between two different levels of space, time, or reality (Schmedes 88). If we assume that *Serial* is not primarily a dramatic production, the use of the police audio alone would have been enough to indicate a different time and space. The fact that sound mixing, specifically fading, is used indicates the desire to create dramatic effect or additional meaning; in this case, it is a way to highlight the authority of the narrator's voice. Moreover, the sound mixing creates a multilayered piece that may be more compelling to some listeners because of its professional production value.

Finally, music is a nonverbal component that significantly influences the narrative portrayed in *Serial*. As Huwiler describes, music can have both syntactic and semantic functions in a narrative. The syntactic functions include introducing and ending the episode and bridging between parts of the narrative, while semantic functions include music that accompanies the story or illustrates any number of meanings, including anticipation, commentary, irony, contrast, or alienation (Huwiler, *Erzähl-Ströme* 61). The music in *Serial* is carefully crafted; the theme song in particular is so catchy and distinct that just a few notes of it set the mood and a level of expectation in the listener. This tune has been described as provoking "a Pavlovian response from listeners eager to get their latest hit of the addictive story" (Strecker). Sometimes, this theme music simply fades in and out in the background while Koenig is speaking in order to highlight, for example, more dramatic moments of reflection.[3] I will not go further into *Serial*'s music, as I focus instead on the elements that more concretely authenticate Koenig's storytelling. While music is essential to consider with regard to the narrative's meaning, it is less directly relevant to the conventions under consideration here—namely, the techniques that create the impression of authenticity and demonstrate that *Serial* follows conventions of traditional crime stories.

Truth Claims and Reality Effects

In dealing with storytelling, we are always confronted with the problem of truth: in fiction, we ask whether each claim is true in the context of a fictional storyworld; and, in nonfiction, we ask whether it corresponds to our real world. Koenig herself repeatedly addresses the difficulty in determining what parts of each person's stories are true and how each of those stories fit together with the evidence available for this case. Koenig does not claim to know or to present an authentic version of the story of Hae Min Lee's murder; instead, she narrates the *search* for that authentic version. Koenig does, however, present an authoritative—in distinction to an authentic—version of the story of Hae Min Lee's murder. I view authenticity and authority as connected insofar as Koenig, in order to convey authority, uses a number of devices signaling the authenticity of the story of her search for the truth.

By using the term "authenticity" here, I risk entering far-reaching territory, which includes various scholarly fields and philosophies of representation. As Susanne Knaller explains, when we talk about authenticity today, we talk about many things, including aura, originality, truthfulness, and realness. Moreover, we enter a conversation that has gained a special momentum since the second half of the twentieth century (Knaller, 7). Despite the fact that all of these factors play into the atmosphere produced in *Serial*, I will define here only in brief terms what Koenig is ostensibly seeking and what she presents in her podcast. Regarding the former, she wants to know in a historical sense what really happened on that particular day in January 1999. In my discussion of the latter—namely, how she portrays this search for truth—my use of the idea of authenticity becomes more problematic. I claim that the podcast consistently signals authenticity in a pointing manner, and by this I mean referential authenticity, a rhetorical effect that results from the conventions of media (Knaller 32–33). Authenticity, or its appearance, is the result of conventions of reception of a certain media, of a "reception pact," as Susanne Knaller puts it: "Recognized also as a rhetorical and medial effect, authenticity is able to constitute the credibility of both factual and subjective truth" (33, my translation). We are talking no longer about authenticity in terms of a singular original work of art or the true author of a literary work but rather about effects that are themselves unavoidably simulacra but that nonetheless refer to something we agree has a reference to the real world and legitimizes our ability to talk about a particular moment in history.

Sarah Koenig uses real material to signal the legitimacy of her report, such as her recorded conversations with Adnan Syed, archival court material, and written documents, which she reads out loud. Certain sounds and phrases concretize the realness of the story even when they serve no documentary purpose, as with the scene-setting announcement that is played at the beginning of each episode: "This is a Global Tel-Link prepaid call from Adnan Syed, an inmate at a Maryland correctional facility." Another example comes from Episode 5, in which Koenig and Dana Chivvis, another producer on the show, attempt to make the drive from Woodlawn High School to Best Buy in the twenty-one minutes that the state prosecutor's office claimed was the time frame in which the murder was committed. Koenig narrates their drive after the fact in a voice-over, but we hear the recording of what is presumably the original attempt in the background, with Koenig occasionally halting her narration to let us hear these original sounds: announcements over the high school loudspeaker, the bell, students shouting and talking as they fill the halls, the click as the latch of a car door opens, the car door closing, and traffic noises ("Route Talk," *Serial* 1.5, 23 October 2014, 3:54−6:00). Adding to the suspense and the feeling that we are along for the ride on this race to prove the state prosecutor's timeline wrong, this whole sequence is accompanied by extradiegetic music that resembles the ticking of a clock. We have here a narratological element: the focalization or point of view is meant to be understood as Koenig and Chivvis', and the sound sequences that accompany their car ride and that are mixed with their voices give us an insight into their feelings at the time.[4] We also have an authenticating element: the audio footage from the timed attempt, overlaid with Koenig's narrative. And yet despite how "real" this feels, the audio has been significantly altered, which is obvious not just in the sound mixing but in the fact that when Koenig says, "it's now 2:17; the bell rang at exactly 2:15," it has actually been not two minutes but exactly twenty seconds since the listener heard the bell ring. What we hear then is a kind of literary portrayal of their attempt to recreate the route rather than an exact replay. The listener is certainly aware that the podcast is the result of intense editing, and yet these discrepancies in what seems like a replay of documentary footage are difficult to detect in a single listening.

The effect created by these sound clips of the high school dismissal are related to a phenomenon observed in the realm of realist fiction by Roland Barthes in his essay "The Reality Effect" (1968). Barthes points out rhetorical constructions that he calls "the *referential illusion*," noting that "just when these details are reputed to *denote* the real directly, all that they do—without saying so—is *signify* it" ("Reality" 148, emphasis in original). This is to suggest not that the details presented by Koenig do not have a real-life referent but rather that her telling of history, like literary realism, joins other forms of narrative in its "incessant need to authenticate the 'real'" (Barthes, "Reality" 146). In a different essay, "Historical Discourse" (1967), Barthes examines whether there is any linguistic feature that distinguishes the literary mode appropriate to historical "science" from the mode appropriate to the epic, novel or drama, ultimately finding only the paradox that we believe facts in historical texts to be somehow directly representative of "facts" or "reality," and yet "the 'fact' can only exist linguistically, as a term in discourse" ("Historical" 153). He notes several recurrent traits of history writing but finds that they exist in other literary discourses as well. This very topic was a concern for the nineteenth-century German historian Leopold von Ranke. In order to write historical texts that showed "how it really was" ("*wie es eigentlich gewesen*"), Ranke tried to de-rhetoricize historiographical texts and erase embellishment or stylistic modes that were reminiscent of fiction (Maurer 22). I mention historical narratives here because the endeavor of *Serial* is fairly similar—namely, to uncover the "facts" of a certain historical event. Moreover, Barthes' findings reinforce the point that rhetorical strategies are shared by fictional and nonfictional narratives, including the use of "reality effects" created by details that are themselves nonfunctional except to "say nothing but this: *we are the real*" (Barthes, "Reality" 148, emphasis in original), and the use "archive effects" such as collecting, naming, and cataloguing—essentially simulating the historian's archival work of collecting and piecing together authentic sources (Maurer 44). We see effects such as these in detective fiction, for instance. The reader is both presented with a self-aware detective (like a historian examining the evidence in an objective manner) and encouraged to take on the role of a detective while reading. In "The Origin of the Detective Novel" (1974), Richard Alewyn traces the origins of the detective novel to the empiricism and logic of the nineteenth century, writing that the detective novel is precisely a model of this era's attempts to "explain reality by methodically collecting and logically ordering facts" (68). This practice applies to both historical and fictional writing in the nineteenth century and has continued to the present. *Serial* shows us that the same techniques can be employed in an oral narrative.

One of the often-discussed questions surrounding Koenig's reporting style concerns her degree of bias and whether objectivity is necessary in this kind of program. In his book on radio journalism, Tim Crook discusses the impossibility of true objectivity but thinks that, since journalists are going to give subjective reports either way, they should at least aim to achieve "a certain standard of subjectivity" (41). He gives an example in which journalists fail to live up to this standard, citing British media and government authorities who refer to race issues as "problem" issues. This language belies their attitude that the problem is the presence of nonwhites rather the attitudes of whites toward nonwhites (Crook 42). Crook cites a 1996 statement by National Public Radio (NPR) in the United States that obliges journalists not to introduce bias into their reporting (44). Yet he also notes the growing tendency toward editorializing on the part of radio journalists. *Serial* is a specific kind of programming that has different standards of objectivity than news reporting. In fact, Koenig often comments on the difficulty of remaining without bias, saying that she swings widely between what she believes about Syed's guilt or innocence. Why should *Serial* thematize this problem of bias in a show that never claims to be impartial? One reason is that creating a guise of objectivity is central to the story regardless of what Koenig says to the contrary. Koenig lays out the "facts" in a way that encourages listeners to treat the series like detective fiction. Her matter-of-fact tone gives the impression that she is showing both sides to every story, as when she constructs each hypothetical scenario only to present counterevidence that negates it. Even Koenig's reportage on her own varying beliefs contributes to a sense of objectivity, helping the listeners to judge the facts—even these facts—for themselves. This convincing guise of objectivity persuades listeners to play the role of the detective themselves—as crime story readers are invariably encouraged to do.

Crime Fiction Conventions

Serial is not fiction. But I am not the first to argue that it nonetheless employs conventions of crime fiction. Crime writer Megan Abbott refers to "the unreliable, emotional narrator that you have in Sarah Koenig, who is a character in her own right in the podcast" (Abbott, 03:43). I will first focus on Koenig as an unreliable narrator and then move to the issue of her own emotional responses to the story. It is certainly true that Koenig does not always reveal all of the information she has on any given subject in any given episode. Episodes often end with cliffhangers and teasers about what is yet to come. Abbott is one of many to point out this issue, and it may well have misled many listeners and certainly raises ethical issues, which I discuss below. Whereas Abbott compares Koenig to a fictional detective as narrator, Hanna Rosin discusses how Koenig appeals to a different tradition to get listeners to trust her. She points out that "Koenig uses all the conventions we've been trained to trust and respond to by *TAL* [*This American Life*] host Ira Glass." The two views need not be in conflict with one another. Koenig's narrative voice is a combination of trustworthy public radio personality and detective sleuth, which makes her an unreliable narrator at times. The concept of the unreliable narrator was coined by Wayne Booth in *The Rhetoric of Fiction* (1961) and generally refers to narrators of fictional texts. The fact that one is dealing with an unreliable narrator can become clear to the reader either immediately or only after some time, as when a "twist" in the story reveals the reader has been misled. But even if deceptive narrators might also be unreliable narrators, the latter are normally not simply lying but making "stronger demands on the reader's powers of inference than do reliable narrators" (Booth 159). Ultimately, unreliable narrators make it more difficult to conceive of a unified story world.

Monika Fludernik and Greta Olson point out that terms such as "unreliable narrator," "implied author," "focalization," and even "author" and "narrator" are no longer understood universally but instead context-dependent and historically variable. Booth's definition of the unreliable narrator has been reconceptualized, in particular by reader-response studies that have demonstrated "that the perception of unreliability is dependent not only on textual signals but also on the reader's cognitive gap-filling activity, on schemata of experience as well as on historical variables" (Fludernik and Olson 3). Readers' judgments of a narrator's reliability depend, therefore, on their expectations of the kind of narrative they are reading and their knowledge of certain conventions. For example, inaccurate or embellished historical fiction would not necessarily be considered an example of an unreliable narrator, just as the reader of a tall tale cannot exactly claim to have been lied to. A completely fantastical story can also still have a reliable narrator, as Wolfgang Riedel suggests (81). In nonfiction, however, we are led to believe that the storyworld is identical to what we accept as our own "real" world. This is the case with *Serial*, for instance, and in autobiographies, as described by Philippe Lejeune in "The Autobiographical Contract." An analysis of the reliability of *Serial*'s narrator presents a unique challenge because the podcast is a relatively new form of media and listeners might not know exactly what to expect. Listeners who associate it with the journalistic endeavors of NPR would be likely to start with the assumption that the narrator is reliable and unbiased. Listeners who pick up on the cues that the podcast is meant to tell a good story, however, may assume that Koenig is withholding information or preparing a twist ending. There was no surprise ending to the series, but the producers chose carefully when to introduce details and individuals. And Koenig's occasional acknowledgement of her own bias does not preclude her from being an unreliable narrator. To the contrary, her admissions and apparently spontaneous utterances were intentionally worked into the show.

Abbott notes how Koenig reveals her own thought patterns and displays a "giddiness that most reporters would conceal when they finally wrote a piece" (Abbott, 04:00). Koenig's casual tone and willingness to reveal her own thought process might make her seem like a more reliable narrator to some listeners, due to her perceived openness. Although Abbott notes that it is not new for reporters to lay out their process in the manner that Koenig does, she points out how the story construction is aligned with typical traits of crime fiction, especially with the cliffhangers and suspense that come with each new episode. Along these same lines, Abbott and others have pointed out the ways in which Koenig emerges as a character in her own podcast. For example, in one of several articles to suggest that Koenig, a white journalist, presents two minority communities in a less than thoughtful—even stereotypical—manner, Jay Caspian Kang writes that "Koenig emerges as the subject as the show's drama revolves not so much around the crime, but rather, her obsessions with it." Here we begin to see the ethical issues around the narrator of a real story becoming more central than the people she portrays, especially if the podcast veers too close to entertainment to be respectful toward those who have and may have suffered injustice.

Another ethical issue relates to how Koenig selectively reveals information as she goes along. She emphasizes the live-investigation format, telling us that the investigation is not yet finished as the reporting begins and that she herself does not know how the story will end. This itself is an ethical problem because Koenig cannot know whether she might make a false assumption about someone that she will have to rescind later, nor does she know how listening to the podcast could affect the people involved with the case, thereby influencing their answers in later interviews with Koenig or even in further legal proceedings. But the fact that Koenig's research is ongoing is not the only reason for the holes in the narrative. Many are intentionally left open and filled in later for narrative effect. Jane Kirtley, professor of media ethics and law at the University of Minnesota, points out how *Serial* differs from traditional investigative journalism on this point: "taking this narrative approach raises a fundamental question, which is, how candid are you being with your audience about what you knew and when you knew it?" (Dockterman). It is beyond the scope of this chapter to investigate whether Koenig intentionally withheld relevant information in order to create suspense at the expense of individuals' reputations. However, the auditory cues and literary techniques employed by *Serial* do suggest an attempt to create suspense in other ways, which aligns the podcast with other forms of crime storytelling.

Conclusion

A defining trait of the podcast is that it is a purely auditory medium and therefore shares many properties with oral storytelling. The podcast's most notable difference, however, is its lack of live interaction. As listeners, we are not part of an interactive relationship in which we provide questions, requests for explanation, and interjections such as laughter; nor are we privy to the gestures or facial expressions of the narrator.[5] Nonetheless, the *Serial* podcasts are constructed in such a way that the listener does feel like a listener in an oral storytelling situation. The podcast often includes Koenig's seemingly spontaneous responses and the appearance of unscripted musings. A possible task of further research might be to examine the affinities between the podcast and oral storytelling traditions. Of particular relevance to the present study would be the nature of credibility in oral storytelling situations that are purely auditory. One could study several aspects relating to *Serial* in particular: how is Koenig's credibility judged as compared to the credibility of other individuals whom she interviews? Do listeners react differently to moments in the podcast that seem more scripted as opposed to apparently spontaneous responses—whether Koenig's or others'? And what effect does the lack of visual input have on believability? Unlike with the visual medium of a television show or movie, in which the constructedness of the medium is visually apparent, listeners of *Serial* might forget that the podcast is a carefully prepared presentation that includes not only the voice of the narrator but a number of other verbal and nonverbal cues that are professionally assembled into a believable and captivating narrative.

Within the first two minutes of Episode 1 of *Serial*, Koenig says, "I'm not a detective or a private investigator. I've not even a crime reporter" ("The Alibi" 01:15). And, yet, she introduces the premise of the story by saying, "Here's the case I've been working on." This is one of the subtle ways in which we are encouraged to see her as a detective and, more subtly, as a character akin to the fictional detective figure. At the same time, Koenig provides an abundance of factual information and auditory cues that place this story squarely in the realm of reality. I have suggested that many of these signals go beyond simply conveying information and instead serve the goal of making the story both entertaining and credible. That is to say that *Serial* is essentially an artistic endeavor and demonstrates that even journalistic reporting can be concerned as much with signifying authenticity as with conveying information.

Notes

1. See, for example, "Audionarratology: Interfaces of Sound and Narrative," International and Interdisciplinary Conference held at Paderborn University, Germany, 11–12 September 2014, organized by Jarmila Mildorf and Till Kinzel, Web, 10 Mar. 2015, <http://www.narratology.net/node/240>. Less recent but noteworthy is Terry R. Hamblin's praise of Tim Crook's *Radio Drama: Theory and Practice* (1999) for its attention to sound theory in its attempt "to redress the lack of contemporary scholarship on radio drama" (184).

2. I am alluding here to an influential model for objective historiography introduced by Leopold von Ranke in nineteenth-century Germany, which I discuss further later in this chapter. His claim that history should be portrayed "*wie es eigentlich gewesen*" ("as it actually was") appeared in the preface to his *Geschichten der romanischen und germanischen Völker* (*Histories of the Roman and Germanic Peoples* [1824]) and has been much debated since (Ranke 4).
3. This happens for about forty-five seconds at minute 38 in Episode 1. About fifteen seconds after the music starts, Koenig shifts to general reflections on why she has gotten involved in this case. Then she resumes talking about the particular issue she is following up on, and the music fades out.
4. Cf. Huwiler's ("Storytelling by Sound" 54) analysis of focalization in *Das Atelierfest* (*The Studio Party*).
5. These properties of face-to-face narration are pointed out by Marie-Laure Ryan in order to make a distinction between oral storytelling in a conversational context versus various modes of interactive narrativity in digital media ("Face-to-Face" 41).

Works Cited

Abbott, Megan. Interview by Todd Zwillich. *The Takeaway*. Podcast audio. 19 Nov. 2014. Web. 26 June 2015. <http://www.podtrac.com/pts/redirect.mp3/audio.wnyc.org/takeaway/takeaway111914-serial.mp3>

Alewyn, Richard. "The Origin of the Detective Novel." In *The Poetics of Murder*. Ed. Glenn W. Most and William W. Stowe. Trans. Glenn W. Most. San Diego: Harcourt, 1983. 62–78. Print.

Barthes, Roland. "Historical Discourse." In *Structuralism: A Reader*. Ed. Michael Lane. Trans. Peter Wexler. London: Jonathan Cape, 1970. 145–155. Print.

———. "The Reality Effect." In *The Rustle of Language*. Ed. and trans. Richard Howard. Berkeley: University of California Press, 1989. 141–18. Print.

Booth, Wayne. *The Rhetoric of Fiction*, 2nd ed. Chicago: University of Chicago Press, 1983. Print.

Bracher, Hans. *Rahmenerzählung und Verwandtes bei G. Keller, C.F. Meyer und T. Storm*. Leipzig: H. Haessel, 1909. Print.

Cassell, Justine and David McNeill. "Gesture and the Poetics of Prose." In *Narrative across Media: The Languages of Storytelling*. Ed. Marie-Laure Ryan. Lincoln: University of Nebraska Press, 2004. 108–137. Print.

Cohn, Dorrit. *The Distinction of Fiction*. Baltimore: The Johns Hopkins University Press, 1999. Print.

Crook, Tim. *International Radio Journalism: History, Theory, and Practice*. London: Routledge, 1998. Print.

Dockterman, Eliana. "How *The Jinx* and *Serial* Strain the Blurry Ethical Lines of Crime Reporting." *Time*. 17 Mar. 2015. Web. 25 Mar. 2016. <http://time.com/3746792/jinx-serial-ethics>

Fludernik, Monika and Greta Olson. "Introduction" to *Current Trends in Narratology*. Ed. Greta Olson. Berlin: De Gruyter, 2011. 1–33. Print.

Hamblin, Terry R. "Radio Drama." *Historical Journal of Film, Radio and Television* 21.2 (2001): 183–185. Web. 1 July 2015. doi:10.1080/01439680120051514.

Herman, David. "Scripts, Sequences, and Stories: Elements of a Postclassical Narratology." *PMLA* 112.5 (1997): 1046–1059. Print.

Huwiler, Elke. *Erzähl-Ströme im Hörspiel: Zur Narratologie der elektroakustischen Kunst*. Paderborn: Mentis, 2005. Print.

———. "Storytelling by Sound: A Theoretical Frame for Radio Drama Analysis." *The Radio Journal* 3.1 (2005): 45–59. Web. 5 Mar. 2015. doi:10.1386/rajo.3.1.45/1.

Jackson, Bruce. *The Story Is True: The Art and Meaning of Telling Stories*. Philadelphia: Temple University Press, 2007. Print.

Kang, Jay Caspian. "White Reporter Privilege." *The Awl*. 13 Nov. 2014. Web. 30 June 2015. <http://www.theawl.com/2014/11/serial-and-white-reporter-privilege>

Knaller, Susanne. *Ein Wort aus der Fremde: Geschichte und Theorie des Begriffs Authentizität*. Heidelberg: Universitätsverlag Heidelberg, 2007. Print.

Koenig, Sarah. *Serial*. Season 1. 3 Oct.–18 Dec. 2014. Web. 3 Mar. 2015. <http://serialpodcast.org>

Lejeune, Philippe. "The Autobiographical Contract." In *French Literary Theory Today*. Ed. Tzvetan Todorov. Trans. R. Carter. Cambridge: Cambridge University Press, 1982. 192–222. Print.

Maurer, Kathrin. *Discursive Interaction: Literary Realism and Academic Historiography in Nineteenth-Century Germany*. Heidelberg: Synchron, 2006. Print.

Mildorf, Jarmila and Till Kinzel, organizers. "Audionarratology: Interfaces of Sound and Narrative." International and Interdisciplinary Conference held at Paderborn University, Germany, 11–12 Sept. 2014. Web. 10 Mar. 2015 <http://www.narratology.net/node/240>

Ranke, Leopold von. *Geschichte der germanischen Völker*. Ed. Willy Andreas. Essen: Phaidon, 1996. Print.

Riedel, Wolfgang. "Das Wunderbare im Realismus." In *Die Dinge und die Zeichen*. Ed. Sabine Schneider and Barbara Hunfeld. Würzburg: Königshausen & Neumann, 2008. 73–94. Print.

Rosin, Hanna. "The Real Secret of *Serial*." *Slate*. 23 Oct. 2014. Web. 2 July 2015. <http://www.slate.com/articles/arts/culturebox/2014/10/serial_podcast_and_storytelling_does_sarah_koenig_think_adnan_syed_is_innocent.html>

Ryan, Marie-Laure. "Face-to-Face Narration." In *Narrative across Media: The Languages of Storytelling*. Ed. Marie-Laure Ryan. Lincoln: University of Nebraska Press, 2004. 41–46. Print.

———. "Introduction" to *Narrative across Media: The Languages of Storytelling*. Ed. Marie-Laure Ryan. Lincoln: University of Nebraska Press, 2004. 1–40. Print.

Ryan, Marie-Laure and Jan-Noël Thon. "Introduction" to *Storyworlds across Media: Toward a Media-Conscious Narratology*. Ed. Marie-Laure Ryan and Jan-Noël Thon. Lincoln: University of Nebraska Press, 2014. 1–21. Print.

Schmedes, Götz. *Medientext Hörspiel: Ansätze einer Hörspielsemiotik am Beispiel der Radioarbeiten von Alfred Behrens*. Münster: Waxmann, 2002. Print.

Strecker, Erin. "How Did 'Serial' Find Its Music? Thank Nick Thorburn." *Billboard*. 24 Nov. 2014. Web. 2 July 2015. <http://www.billboard.com/articles/news/6327664/serial-podcast-music-nick-thorburn>

Todorov, Tzvetan. "The Typology of Detective Fiction." In *The Poetics of Prose*. Trans. Richard Howard. Ithaca, NY: Cornell University Press, 1977. Print.

3 Narrative Levels, Theory of Mind, and Sociopathy in True-Crime Narrative—Or, How Is *Serial* Different from Your Average *Dateline* Episode?

David Letzler

In the 1990s, a teenaged girl in a coastal minority community—bright and hardworking, popular in her social circle—disappears one day. There is a frantic search, especially focused on locating the victim's missing car. Eventually, her dead body is discovered. Suspicion falls upon an ex-lover, angered by the victim's new romantic relationship. There is little physical evidence to directly link him to the crime, though, and there are problems in establishing his precise timeline, particularly regarding how his story lines up with that of a possible accomplice. Some in the community are unsatisfied with how the case is initially treated, but, years later, fresh developments emerge, leading to renewed legal proceedings in 2015.

This is a more-or-less accurate description of the story told in the first season of *Serial*. But it's also a fair description of "The Promise," a 2015 episode of *Dateline* about the death of Placentia, California, college student Cathy Torrez. *Dateline* is a long-running network institution with an audience of millions, but "The Promise" did not create nearly the national sensation that *Serial* did. There were no think pieces or fan communities dedicated toward Torrez and her convicted killer, ex-boyfriend Sam Lopez. "The Promise" seems to have been received like most true-crime journalism stories: a suspenseful narrative adequate to fill a Sunday night, but somewhat conventional and melodramatic. It may be a heartening demonstration of how justice prevails over time, but it's not worth thinking about long after it airs.

If you ever need to provide an example of the importance of narrative (*sjužet*) over story (*fabula*), look no further than *Serial*.[1] The basic events in the murder of Hae Min Lee and the arrest of Adnan Syed are, fundamentally, no different from that of a crime-of-the-week special. The parallels between the cases, of course, are not infinite: Syed was tried and convicted shortly after the murder, with *Serial* prompting new hearings on his possible innocence, while Lopez was released after his first arrest and not convicted until

2015; for that matter, the most damning evidence against Syed came from his alleged accomplice, Jay Wilds, while Lopez's assistant, a cousin named Xavier, provided the accused's alibi and stuck to it for decades. But my point is not about this specific *Dateline* episode. It's that I found a *Dateline* episode whose basic story aligns with *Serial*'s within about ten minutes of browsing the show's website. There are, doubtless, many more examples in the archives of the nation's true-crime journalism shows.

Anyone who believes that the chief distinguishing characteristic of Sarah Koenig's podcast, then, is that it uncovered an inherently compelling story is mistaken. Think of how easy it would be to reconceive the Lee case as a *Dateline* episode. One can picture the interviews with Hae's family, tearily providing quotidian details to humanize her loss; the grainy reenactments of a car being driven to Leakin Park and a body later being found behind a fallen tree; the gruff police officers explaining their investigative process; and so on. If *Dateline* were to have gotten the story first, I would wager that the NPR audience who doted on *Serial* would view the murder more or less as it does those in most true-crime TV episodes: compelling as far as it goes, but a little tawdry, and not worthy of the kind of solemn soul-searching *Serial* provoked.

Certainly, the reality of both the Lee murder and the long-term incarceration of Syed are of life-and-death importance to those directly affected, as are the death of Torrez and the conviction of Lopez. I do not want to diminish the seriousness of the actual events, as distinct from their telling. There has been considerable public debate about the ethics of how *Serial* turns a real murder case into morning-run listening (see Goldstein), and that problem extends to true-crime shows generally. I do not have space here to engage this issue fully, except to point out that, as a literary critic, I resist the notion that presenting something as dramatic narrative necessarily trivializes it. My point is simply that, for the broader audience captivated by *Serial*, its appeal rests within the narrative construction, not the events of the murder.

In this chapter, then, I want to provide a detailed narrative analysis of what makes *Serial*'s structure so compelling, contrasting it with the *Dateline* episode. In particular, I will use the classic system of narrative levels laid out by Gérard Genette, as well as the more recent system of embedded conscious levels articulated by Lisa Zunshine, to show the intricate layering in *Serial*'s narrative as compared to *Dateline*'s. Furthermore, I want to show how *Serial* presents a complication to Zunshine's "mind-reading" model in its invocation, as the series progresses, of the possibility of psychopathy in the narrative's major characters. That complication, I believe, gets to the heart of why *Serial* is so compelling, but it also reveals its single biggest failing.

*

Serial has sometimes been described as a two-level narrative—"just as much the story of Koenig's reporting as it is the story of Hae's murder" (Goldstein). This description, however, considerably undersells it. There are at least four narrative levels to *Serial*. In Gérard Genette's classic formulation, a narrative level is defined by its "narrating instance," or how its specific narrative situation relates rhetorically to the story that is recounted (213–216). Narratives may be stacked at multiple levels if a story being told itself incorporates a narrating instance, as in *One Thousand and One Nights* (227–231). Genette argues that there is always at least one distinction in level because even something as intimate as a daily diary entry implies its author existing on two levels: as the protagonist in the brief narrative and as the narrator who recounts what happened to that character at a remove (228). However, for a level to be clearly distinguished, there must be some rhetorical distance established between it and the others. For instance, distinct levels are nearly effaced in stream-of-consciousness narration (218–219) and some forms of omniscient/undramatized narration (220–221). By contrast, in many stories, the rhetorical relationship between levels is developed to a point where it becomes one of the central elements of the narrative, as in *Wuthering Heights* (217).

The first level distinction set up in *Serial* is, crucially, not the distinction between Hae's murder and Koenig's investigation but the subtler one between the January murder and the police investigation throughout February and March. In her opening comments, Koenig speaks with her teenage nephew's social circle and discovers that none of them can quite recall what they had been doing on the Friday afternoon six weeks prior (e.g., "I would be in school—actually, I think I worked that day" [*Serial* I-1]). At a remove of even that much time, we are sufficiently alienated from who we were then that we can no longer reliably recount what we were doing. Typically, of course, most of what we forget is not important and hence not worth reflecting upon later anyway. However, as *Serial* illustrates, there are occasions when those forgotten periods become important, as when suspects in a murder investigation must recall what they were doing some time before. For example, the alibi Adnan gave to the police was, "When school was over, I would have went to the library," yet we learn from his friend Rabia Chaudry (who initially involves Koenig in the case) that he had told her, "She disappeared in January, you know? In March, you're asking me, like, where were you after school for 20 minutes on a specific day? All the days are the same to me, you know?" (*Serial* I-1). Consequently, we must consider not only the stories told by the case's participants but the positions from which they were narrated after the fact.

Serial's investigation adds a third layer, since even more has been lost to memory in the fifteen years since the initial investigation. Koenig, for instance, spends much of the first episode telling us about the letters written to Adnan by Asia McClain on March 1–2, 1999, offering to corroborate Adnan's alibi for January 13. Much of this passage, though, foregrounds Koenig's own narration about these letters, due to the efforts she must go through with Rabia to locate Asia and puzzle out the reason Asia's testimony was not sought out by (now-deceased) attorney Cristina Gutierrez for Adnan's defense. So, as listeners, we must navigate between (A) Koenig's investigation into (B) the initial investigation into (C) the murder itself.

The fourth level is the subtlest, but, if we attend to the narrating situations, we can make it out. Frequently, Koenig's conversations with the key figures in the Lee case, recorded at various points in 2013 and 2014, are interspersed with her later reflections about those interviews, spoken while editing the materials for the podcast in late 2014. This might seem like a trivial distinction, but, in *Serial*, it is an important one. For instance, after Koenig implores Asia to bring her testimony before a judge and Asia merely sighs, we hear Koenig tell us, "And I completely understand that sigh. I feel that way a lot of the time" (*Serial* I-1). Though the audio transitions seamlessly, we have changed levels, with the interviewer's relentless advocacy switching to the editor's introspective reflection. In short, within the first episode, we have already established four narrative levels: (A) Koenig talking to us in 2014 about how she feels about (B) what she's talked about to her interviewees over the past year regarding (C) what they had said about the investigation in February and March 1999 about (D) what they had done around the time of the murder in January 1999.[2]

This is an unusual approach to the genre. The narrative of "The Promise," for example, never rises above three narrative levels, tends to stick to two, and often goes out of its way to streamline everything into one, no matter how unnatural that structure may be. This decision has nothing to do with the actual temporal complexity of the investigation, since the Torrez case covers a longer period of time than the Lee case—1994–2015, as opposed to 1998–2014—and was more multi-staged. Little of consequence happened in the Lee case between the year 2000 and the beginning of Koenig's investigation, while the Torrez case—propelled by the persistent work of detective Daron Wyatt—produced periodic progress after the original investigation: the initial arrest of Xavier (who was released) in 1997, the arrest of Sam in 1999 (who, again, was released), the D.A. office's decision to retackle the case in 2003, the second arrest of Sam and Xavier in 2007, and a trial in 2015. But "The Promise" presents these events in close to chronological order. With the exception of a few investigative passages reconstructing Sam's involvement with Cathy and some jolting juxtapositions of mid-1990s photos of the Lopez family with their 2015 mug shots, little is made of the relationship between the case's temporal layers.

That seems deliberate, because the program employs several stylistic tics to flatten the narrative. The lead on-camera investigator, Josh Mankiewicz, frequently employs an interview strategy that, while typical of true-crime reports, is utterly bizarre when contemplated from a narrative perspective: restating the essence of what an interviewee has just said, but in the present tense. Consider this passage, when Cathy's mother, Mary Bennett, recounts phoning to the police that Cathy is missing:

MANKIEWICZ: And the police said . . .?

BENNETT: "Well, you know, you don't know that. Maybe she went off and . . ." But I knew that—

MANKIEWICZ: "She could have met some guy and they're in Vegas right now." And you're saying, "Not possible."

BENNETT: At that point, you want to yell and scream at them and tell them, "That's not true. You don't know. Not my Cathy."

Note Mankiewicz's transition from the past-tense "said" to the present-tense "are saying," which induces Mary to move from the past-tense "knew" to the present "want." Mankiewicz is not trying to highlight the multiple levels here, à la *Serial*. On the contrary, by ventriloquizing Mary's thoughts from twenty-one years prior into his own present-tense person rather than letting Mary recount them at a distance, he collapses three different levels (the interview, the investigation, the murder) into one. It's as if he wants to evoke the collaborative spirit in the pursuit of justice while erasing the temporal difference that such a collaboration requires. "The Promise" seems to want to give its viewers the impression that they are experiencing the murder and investigation as they unfold rather than retracing it from a distance.

We can observe the cost of that visceral appeal by using Lisa Zunshine's model of embedded levels of narrated consciousness. Zunshine's approach is based on the concept of Theory of Mind, or "mind-reading," the process by which we project from others' physical behavior or speech an entire conscious state, even though we do not have direct access to it. As Zunshine notes, literary fiction not only requires us to use our Theory of Mind but frequently does so at multiple levels. For instance, regarding one passage of *Mrs. Dalloway*, Zunshine notes that "Richard *suspects* that Lady Bruton indeed *believes* that because, as Hugh *says*, the makers of the pen *think* that it will never wear out, the editor of the *Times* will *respect* and publish the ideas recorded by this pen" (33), involving five embedded levels of consciousness. Zunshine generally argues that popular fiction tends not to go beyond four levels, while literary texts often exceed that total (38).

Serial takes advantage of its four narrative levels to stack many layers of embedded consciousness. This is nowhere more evident than in Koenig's fraught interviews with Adnan, which involve not only his (apparent) attempt to read his own memories but Koenig's worries about how far to trust him and how far to press her search. This comes to a head toward the end of the penultimate episode, where Adnan writes Koenig a long letter expressing the worries he's had about his case being so publicly reopened. After reading his description of finding peace in prison, Koenig tells us,

> And now I come along—at Rabia's behest, not his—and yank this door open again to the outside world and to all its doubts about Adnan's integrity, stirring up the most painful possible questions about whether he's a monster. It's his nightmare, basically, to be accused of manipulating everyone around him.
>
> (*Serial* I-11)

In this passage, we hear (1) Koenig's guilt about (2) Adnan's anxiety over (3) Rabia's initial interest in enlisting, and ensuing national curiosity about, (4) Koenig's eager investigative efforts to figure out whether (5) Adnan's 2014 expressions of innocence reflect (6) his February 1999 self's true attitude regarding (7) his friends' belief that (8) his January 13, 1999, self was not involved in Hae's death. It's an incredibly complex moment.

No such moments occur anywhere in "The Promise." Because the story is so resolutely chronological, the interviewees are often only able to express the single conscious state they possessed at a given point in the investigation. There are few probing questions about their judgment, and there is certainly no self-examination of Mankiewicz's own activities. For instance, at one point, Wyatt points out that Sam had "[n]o criminal history. There was [*sic*] no indicators that he was anything other than, you know, a normal twenty-two-year-old kid." And Mankiewicz answers, "He doesn't sound like a killer." Here, Mankiewicz is not merely ventriloquizing Wyatt's speech but embodying his former consciousness, effacing the difference between his mind, Wyatt's current mind, and Wyatt's mind from eighteen years prior. Again, the aim appears to be to give the audience the sensation of being immediately in the story. The only significant moment of embedding occurs in the opening passage (recalled at the episode's end), when Mary tells Mankiewicz how she still wakes up at 3:40 am, the time the police informed her Cathy's body had been found. "For the last twenty-one years," he tells us in voiceover, "that particular time has stabbed her in the heart, pulled her awake," at which point he segues into Tina Torrez's description of Cathy's cheery personality. I see four embedded states here: (1) Mankiewicz's somber introduction of (2) Mary's lingering heartache over (3) her younger self's panicked anguish about realizing she might never see (4) her daughter's joyous smile again. That's about as intricate as "The Promise" gets.

*

It may be objected at this point that I have, so far, willfully overlooked the biggest difference between the two murders. The Lee case, a *Serial* fan might argue, is a far more complex mystery than the Torrez case. The Torrez case, after all, wrapped up neatly with Sam's conviction, while *Serial*'s investigation into the Lee case revealed myriad evidentiary holes. The real interest in *Serial*, they might argue, is in the complexities of the evidence. As plausible as this argument might sound, though, I think it is more a sign of the effectiveness of *Serial*'s narrative technique than anything about the case itself. Despite all appearances, the major evidence in the Torrez and Lee murders is not all that different.

I want to be clear that I am going to limit my discussion to evidence referenced in *Serial* and "The Promise." Obviously, mountains of information have been collected regarding both cases, and only a small amount is presented on either program. But our main question is why so many people became invested in the former program rather than the latter, which, for many, derived from the show's argument that Adnan was wrongly convicted (see Larson). Moreover, we can assume that *Serial*, in the name of creating an interesting narrative, would present the most compelling information it could find to cast doubt on Adnan's guilt. Certainly, it did well to undermine some parts of the state's account: between Koenig and producer Dana Chivvis's retracing of the timeline in Jay's official story (*Serial* I-5) and the show's interview with Hae's friend Summer, who says Hae was talking with her in the gym at the moment the police believed the murder occurred (*Serial* I-9), the show did excellent work in demonstrating that the story presented at trial is not plausible. Yet that is not the same as making a convincing case against Adnan's guilt. I am going to assert something now that might take *Serial*'s fans aback: based on the evidence presented in *Serial*, I find little reason to doubt Adnan's guilt.

Here is why. The only inescapable piece of evidence directly linking anyone to the murder—as acknowledged by both Koenig (*Serial* I-4, I-12) and Jim Trainum, the independent investigator she hires to audit their work (*Serial* I-8)—is Hae's car. After it had remained missing for weeks, Jay told the police the location of Hae's car and led them to it (*Serial* I-4). What's more, Jennifer Pusateri claims Jay had confessed to being involved in Hae's death on the day of the killing (*Serial* I-4), which means Jay probably did not find the car after the fact but was linked, in some way, to the murder. No one, however, has provided any kind of plausible motive Jay might have had either for killing Hae or for assisting someone other than Adnan in doing so. Furthermore, while Adnan's exact timeline on the day of Hae's disappearance is disputed, it is not in dispute that he spent at least some significant part of the afternoon and evening with Jay (*Serial* I-1, I-2, I-4, I-5)—despite the fact that, even though Adnan claims to have loaned his car and phone to Jay, he tells Koenig that he and Jay weren't close friends (*Serial* I-4).

These basic facts can be accounted for by only two classes of possibilities. In one, Jay is part of a planned conspiracy (since he could not have simultaneously driven both Adnan's and Hae's cars alone) that kills Hae and sets up an innocent Adnan for reasons unknown. In the other, things went more or less as Jay claims, albeit on a different timeline than he presented in court and perhaps with a different level of involvement on his part. The first option, while not completely impossible, is wholly unsubstantiated. Jay and/or some acquaintance might have had some hidden reason to kill Hae, but, given that the whole of both Gutierrez's defense (*Serial* I-8) and Koenig's podcast depend upon the possibility of Jay's guilt, the fact that neither managed to find any reason why Jay might've wanted to set up Adnan leaves us with no basis to credit this possibility. While the second possibility has holes, none are insurmountable. Hae might have been killed later in the day, with Jay either mistaken or lying about the timeline. It is easily the more plausible solution.

The *Serial* team more or less acknowledges this point in the final episode. Chivvis points out that Adnan would have been "ridiculously unlucky" to have innocently offered his phone and car to someone who would use them to frame him for murder (*Serial* I-12)—not to mention that the additional car would have logistically complicated any preexisting conspiracy against him. Koenig subsequently acknowledges that her team may have "appl[ied] excessive scrutiny to a perfectly ordinary case" (*Serial* I-12), yet she insists that the crime specialists they spoke to (including Trainum) assured them that "this case is a mess" (*Serial* I-12). In her closing remarks, Koenig belittles the importance of Hae's car and claims that, were she on a jury, she would not vote to convict Adnan (*Serial* I-12). However, she cannot quite bring herself to say she believes in his innocence—likely, I suspect, because she doesn't have any plausible story that explains Jay's knowledge of the car without Adnan's guilt.

And tellingly, in "The Promise," a similar line of argument is all that is needed to convict Sam. When the case finally comes to trial, Sam's attorney points out, like Koenig, the absence of direct evidence linking the accused to the crime. The real evidence, he notes, is against the accomplice Xavier, whose DNA was found on the car by the crime lab years later. But, as the prosecution argues, Xavier had no motive to kill Cathy, and, moreover, Sam's alibi for the time of her death was that he had spent the evening with Xavier. The winning formula for the prosecution, then, is that the evidence of the car implicated Xavier, Xavier had been with Sam during the time of the murder, and Sam had the motive. Replace "Xavier" with "Jay" and "Sam" with "Adnan," and the argument maps over quite neatly. Yes, there is some DNA evidence in the Torrez case, and there are some holes in Jay's account of the killing. But those holes are present because the police *had a confession from Jay*, which the Placentia police did not have from Xavier. Altogether, the case against Adnan is comparably strong to the case against Sam.

So why were so many *Serial* listeners convinced the Lee case was so complex? The issue, I suspect, comes back to the intricate mind-reading processes that the show asks its readers to perform. Because we must navigate eight levels of hypothesized mental states during the Koenig-Adnan dialogues, *Serial* listeners come to feel a rich sense of Adnan's interiority. Since his voice over the prison phone is his only way to reach the outside world, in fact, we may feel we have a responsibility to do so. Meanwhile, we get no opportunity to undergo the same process with Jay, who defends his privacy and refuses to let his brief interview be recorded (*Serial* I-8). All that we know is that his story has many inconsistencies, muddying our ability to understand him. Even Jay's friend Cathy, in the process of defending him, says, "Jay lies. That's why he does that. Jay lies about everything" (*Serial* I-8). That leads to two different tendencies in our natural mind-reading apparatus: Adnan comes off as transparent; Jay, as opaque. When Koenig hears that Jay claimed Adnan had talked to him after the murder (about "all the other motherfuckers, referring to like hoods and thugs and stuff, [who] think they're hardcore. But he just killed a person with his bare hands"), she recoils (*Serial* I-11). She apparently has more trouble imagining Adnan would speak like that than imagining he would commit the murder. Even though the evidentiary logic implicates Adnan, then, our default mind-reading practices make us warier of Jay.

That tension is, perhaps, *Serial*'s most fascinating attribute. In normal circumstances, we do admirably well in inferring others' minds from what little information we have to work with: usually, you can look at a stranger's face on the street and tell whether that person is currently happy, distracted, or miserable. But while this ability often makes us think we have easy access to others' minds, we do not. As Zunshine notes, when we are analyzing a mystery, in which there is a strong possibility we are being deceived about others' mental states, the cognitive strain of performing multilevel mind-reading increases substantially, as does the possibility for error (130–132).[3] And our brains have a particularly strong block toward reading a type of mind disproportionately common in murder cases: the charming psychopath.

Toward the end of *Serial*, Koenig brings up the possibility that some of her interview subjects, especially Adnan, might be psychopaths. To pursue the question, she speaks with criminologist Charles Ewing (*Serial* I-11), but he is of little help. Psychopaths, Ewing tells us, lack "genuine empathy," but they also "come across very smoothly and effectively manipulate other people and manipulate them without them knowing it," such that their lack of empathy is not apparent. They often lie but are "glib," with "superficial charm," so that you don't suspect they're lying. Koenig asks if the fact that Adnan has maintained relationships with people outside the prison and functions well inside it would be inconsistent with psychopathy, and Ewing agrees that it "cuts against" that diagnosis but unhelpfully adds that it "doesn't rule it out." Ewing himself, the expert, admits he's been fooled several times by psychopaths (*Serial* I-11). Koenig resists the characterization of Adnan as a psychopath because she thinks he does show empathy (*Serial* I-11)—but then there is little difference between what an empathetic person sounds like and what a psychopath performing empathy sounds like.

This is a problem that goes well beyond *Serial* itself. As the vagueness of Ewing's description implies, there is very little agreement in psychology and neuroscience about the nature of what is commonly called psychopathy or sociopathy. They are not included in the most recent *Diagnostic and Statistical Manual of Mental Disorders* (DSM-V), for instance. The closest condition is "Anti-Social Personality Disorder," which is characterized by a combination of impulsiveness, deceit, recklessness, and remorselessness (659). What cognitively characterizes such individuals is unclear, except that there is some evidence to suggest the condition is linked to connectivity impairment in the prefrontal cortex (Motzkin et al.). All we really understand is that there exists some percentage of the human population, disproportionately male, who seem generally indifferent to the basic ethical bonds that otherwise undergird society.

Let me offer a hypothesis. When Zunshine imported Theory of Mind to literary studies, she invoked Simon Baron-Cohen's suggestion that autism could be explained as a deficit in Theory of Mind—i.e., that autistic individuals are distinguished by their inability to "mind-read" others (6–12). This viewpoint has since lost favor (cf. Savarese and Zunshine 17). However, if literary criticism wishes a better candidate to define the limit case of our mind-reading capacity, psychopathy might serve. There is some evidence to suggest that individuals flagged as psychopaths score below the average on Theory of Mind tests (Ali and Chamorro-Premuzic). This should not be surprising, given their lack of empathy: if psychopaths are distanced from others' feelings, it makes sense that they might not be able to figure out what goes on in others' heads. However, there are disturbing exceptions. Researchers generally separate empathy into "cognitive" and "emotional" varieties—the former "the ability to *understand* and infer the emotions and emotional experiences of another" (i.e., mind-reading ability) and the latter "the capacity to *experience* the emotions of another" (i.e., intersubjective affective experience) (Ali and Chamorro-Premuzic 169). Unfortunately, there is evidence to suggest that some male psychopaths can improve their cognitive empathy as they mature, even as their emotional empathy remains stunted (Dadds et al.).[4] In other words, they are able to acquire some knowledge about what goes on in others' heads without the burden of having to feel it themselves.

For reasons that may be clear, this makes them extremely dangerous. In recent years, research on mirror neurons has theorized that we humans learn our complex cultural tasks so quickly because, when we observe others perform tasks, some neurons in our brain can actually fire in a way that mimics the firing of the task's performer (Ramachandran 117–135). In other words, to learn how to function in society, our brains must recognize their similarity to the brains of others. Though theory on mirror neurons is still far from settled, it's possible that this process establishes certain ethical controls: if a prerequisite to advanced human functioning is the understanding that others are like us, then there will generally be a negative correlation between our skill at causing harm to others and our willingness to do so because the committer of the harm will empathize too strongly with those who might suffer from it. But this depends upon cognitive and emotional empathy remaining reasonably well associated. That is generally true for neurotypical individuals (Cox et al.), but, when they dissociate to favor cognitive over emotional empathy, there are two serious consequences. First, since a psychopath can figure out how to mimic others' complex behaviors without having to experience something like their subjectivity, the psychopath can learn to pursue his or her goals without the internal moral check that our emotional empathy usually provides. Second, since emotional and cognitive empathy are connected for most of us, it is difficult for us to understand a mind in which they are not. It has been popular recently to conceive of autism not as a global failure of empathy but as an imbalance in which emotional empathy dominates cognitive empathy (Cox et al.), which might explain autistic individuals' desire, but frequent failure, to share others' emotions. Yet as Ralph Savarese notes, for all the difficulty autistics may have in reading neurotypicals, neurotypicals have as much difficulty reading autistics (Saverese and Zunshine 25). The same symmetry, sadly, will not apply to skilled psychopaths, whose cognitive architecture can make it harder for us to read them than for them to read us. Not only can psychopaths act without conscience, then, but they can evade our attempts to figure out what is going on in their heads.

Should that be a concern when we listen to *Serial*? Koenig raises the possibility that Adnan is a sociopath to Innocence Project director Deirdre

Enright, who replies, "The odds of you getting the charming sociopath? You're just not that lucky" (*Serial* I-7). But we shouldn't downplay the likelihood of psychopathy in a murder case, given that some estimates place psychopathy in prison populations at close to twenty-five percent, far higher than their prevalence in the general population (Motzkin et al.). I could tell any of a number of stories to explain why Jay's accounts don't line up but still implicate Adnan. Perhaps Jay was so shocked by seeing Hae's corpse that the day's events became blurred. Perhaps, because he considered himself the school badass, when his square friend showed up with a dead body, he tried to convince himself he was used to this kind of thing and tried not to treat the day as special. Perhaps he and Adnan planned the death together, and, when they were found out, Jay decided his best bet was to give up Adnan and minimize his culpability, while Adnan decided to maintain his innocence. It's impossible to say. Similarly, Adnan could have boasted of being a hardcore killer to Jay without the persona being his "true" one: he might have been performing streetwise toughness to impress Jay, just as he might be performing sincerity to impress Koenig. That's probably part of why Trainum tells Koenig to disregard everything everyone has said about Adnan's apparent mindset at the time of Hae's disappearance (*Serial* I-8): when dealing with possible psychopaths, we are not reliable judges. I am not trying to armchair-diagnose Adnan as a psychopath—not even a trained psychologist could do that at a distance—but I am saying we cannot use our intuitive mind-reading responses to determine whether or not Adnan (or, for that matter, Jay) is one.

Incidentally, we should observe that *Serial*'s treatment of the question of how to mind-read a psychopath is still vastly better than *Dateline*'s. In "The Promise," the D.A.'s office sends specialist Frank Montgomery (a.k.a. "The Evidence Whisperer") to review the Torrez case, and, based on the recorded interviews, he makes a number of bold statements about Sam's mindset. While he offers a few good points (e.g., about the calls to Sam's pager from the Torrez house), most are psychobabble. Montgomery finds it suspicious that Sam can refer to Cathy's disappearance only through indirect phrases like "this happened" (as if no innocent person would want to avoid speaking directly about his ex-lover's death) and that Sam says he doesn't want "memories to come back" about Cathy (as if otherwise happy memories of the recently dead mightn't become painful). Combined with Wyatt's judgment that Sam exhibits insufficient emotion about Cathy's death (as if an innocent person might not try to suppress emotion about a lover's death), this is enough for them to classify Sam as a psychopath. Sam's attorney, rightly, dismantles this line of reasoning.

Yet there is, perhaps, a benefit to the relative simplicity of "The Promise." Near the end of the final episode of *Serial*, Koenig leaves us with a final statement of indeterminacy: "I don't believe any of us can say what really happened to Hae" (*Serial* I-12). It's the kind of comment popular with academics of a postmodern persuasion. It echoes, for instance, literary critic David Cowart's comment (apropos of Don DeLillo's *Libra*) that the evidence on the JFK assassination leaves us only with "irreducible confusion" (97). Koenig is right that we can't get direct experiential access to the events of the past. But, by the same token, I can never really know where my wife spent the hours between eight this morning and five-thirty this evening: it is possible that she, her coworkers, and the government are lying to me about her attendance at work. If I applied that degree of scrutiny to every element of my life, though, I could never get through the day. It's probably why Trainum seems relatively unconcerned about the "bad evidence" in the Lee case (i.e., data that doesn't fit the official theory) (*Serial* I-8): people are unclear or mistaken about little things all the time, and, even at a distance of a few weeks, it becomes difficult to retrieve conclusive proof of the network of causes and effects that lined them all up.

Consider what would happen if we applied Koenig's indeterminacy to "The Promise." As clear-cut as the Torrez case looks, we can find any number of unanswered questions if we increase our scrutiny. For instance, what precisely happened the week before Cathy's murder, when Cathy arrived home distraught, possibly drugged, and without her underwear? What of Albert, the new boyfriend whom we are told killed himself early in the episode but hear almost nothing else about afterward—could the two tragic events, so close together in time, have truly been independent? Even Sam's post-conviction confession can be parsed for doubt because his confession uses the same circuitous phrasing Frank Montgomery warns us about earlier in the episode. Instead of directly saying that he killed her, Sam says, "It was all my fault. [. . .] This was a horrible act that never should have happened." What if he is just covering for the true killer, Xavier, now that his own fate has been sealed? A *Serial*-like account could cast plenty of doubt upon Sam's conviction.

Would we want it to do so? Do we want our legal system to err toward crediting the persistent gaps in our knowledge rather than those things we can reconstruct? Indeterminacy has long been proposed by literary theorists as a tool to dismantle oppressive dominant ideologies, but it is also an effective tool for dismantling accountability: if we believe that knowledge is always a rhetorical construction, that our subjecthoods are contingent rather than autonomous, then we can never hold anyone responsible for anything. Few of the innocent will be subjected to the punishment of our disciplinary system, but the guilty will mostly go free, too. Judith Butler might not mind that, but I would prefer otherwise. I will never be on a jury judging the fate of Adnan Syed or hear the full range of evidence that might be brought to his defense. But, as a listener, I vote to convict him, just as I would Sam.

The first season of *Serial* is an extraordinary narrative achievement. It requires our fullest mental commitments to parse what we can and cannot understand regarding the passage of time, our lapses in memory, and our perceptions of others. The conversations between Koenig and Adnan call forth enormously complicated questions about our ethical obligations and the possible blind spots in our cognitive evaluations. Certainly, it requires far more of our minds than is asked by "The Promise." It is only in the final judgment—that binary decision so hated by post-structuralism, yet so necessary in the real world—that it falls short.

Notes

1. With *Serial* having shown in its first season what innovative narrative technique can do with relatively commonplace story materials, it is ironic that *Serial*'s second season should cover an issue of significant national importance in a relatively straightforward NPR style. In contrast to Season 1, the greater consensus about the sequence of events in Season 2 allows for a relatively straightforward reconstruction: we reach the sixth episode before the series departs from linear chronology in any significant way. Moreover, since Koenig never gets to speak directly to Bowe Bergdahl—and since the journalist Mark Boal, who does interview him, largely believes what he says—there is less opportunity for the fraught layering that characterizes Season 1.
2. To be exactingly precise to Genette's definition, an example of four embedded speakers occurs at the point when Koenig tells us about Rabia telling her about having talked during the investigation to Asia, who recounted what Adnan and Derek had said to her on the day of the murder (*Serial* I-1).
3. However, for reasons that will become clear, I do not entirely agree with Zunshine's subsequent claim: "There are no material clues independent from mind-reading" (133).
4. Dadds et al. resist the equation between their measure of cognitive empathy and Theory of Mind, but only for local reasons. Their particular construct relies upon caregiver reports rather than test subjects' direct mind-reading performance, and the latter is the diagnostic typically used in Theory of Mind experiments (600). I understand their methodological reluctance, but it is likely that the two measures are highly correlated, so, for the purposes of my paper, I am willing to overlook the qualification.

Works Cited

Ali, Farah and Tomas Chamorro-Premuzic. "Investigating Theory of Mind Deficits in Nonclinical Psychopathy and Machiavellianism." *Personality and Individual Differences* 49 (2010): 169–174. Print.

American Psychiatric Association. *Diagnostic and Statistical Manual of Mental Disorders*. 5th ed. Arlington, VA: American Psychiatric Publishing, 2013. Print.

Cowart, David. *Don DeLillo: The Physics of Language*. Athens, GA: University of Georgia Press, 2003. Print.

Cox, Christine et al. "The Balance between Feeling and Knowing: Affective and Cognitive Empathy Reflected in the Brain's Intrinsic Functional Dynamics." *Social Cognitive and Affective Neuroscience* 7.6 (2012): n. pag. Web. 18 Feb. 2016.

Dadds, Mark R. et al. "Learning to 'Talk the Talk': The Relationship of Psychopathic Traits to Deficits in Empathy Across Childhood." *Journal of Child Psychology and Psychiatry* 50.5 (2009): 599–606. Print.

"Episode 01: The Alibi." Narr. Sarah Koenig. *Serial: Season One*. NPR, 3 Oct. 2014. Podcast. 20 Mar. 2015.

"Episode 02: The Breakup." Narr. Sarah Koenig. *Serial: Season One*. NPR, 3 Oct. 2014. Podcast. 23 Mar. 2015.

"Episode 04: Inconsistencies." Narr. Sarah Koenig. *Serial: Season One*. NPR, 16 Oct. 2014. Podcast. 28 Mar. 2015.

"Episode 05: Route Talk." Narr. Sarah Koenig. *Serial: Season One*. NPR, 23 Oct. 2014. Podcast. 31 Mar. 2015.

"Episode 07: The Opposite of the Prosecution." Narr. Sarah Koenig. *Serial: Season One*. NPR, 06 Nov. 2014. Podcast. 5 Apr. 2015.

"Episode 08: The Deal With Jay." Narr. Sarah Koenig. *Serial: Season One*. NPR, 13 Nov. 2014. Podcast. 8 Apr. 2015.

"Episode 11: Rumors." Narr. Sarah Koenig. *Serial: Season One*. NPR, 11 Dec. 2014. Podcast. 16 Apr. 2015.

"Episode 12: What We Know." Narr. Sarah Koenig. *Serial: Season One*. NPR, 18 Dec. 2014. Podcast. 18 Apr. 2015.

Genette, Gérard. *Narrative Discourse*. Trans. Jane E. Lewin. Ithaca: Cornell University Press, 1980. Print.

Goldstein, Jessica. "The Complicated Ethics of *Serial*, the Most Popular Podcast of All Time." *ThinkProgress.org*. Center for American Progress Action Fund, 20 Nov. 2014. Web. 16 Feb. 2016.

Larson, Sarah. "What '*Serial*' Really Taught Us." *NewYorker.com*. Condé Nast, 18 Dec. 2014. Web. 16 Feb. 2016.

Motzkin, Julian C. et al. "Reduced Prefrontal Connectivity in Psychopathy." *The Journal of Neuroscience* 30.48 (2011): n. pag. Web. 18 Feb. 2016.

"The Promise." Narr. Josh Mankiewicz. *Dateline*. NBC. 24 Apr. 2015. Web. 3 Feb. 2016.

Ramachandran, V. S. *The Tell-Tale Brain: A Neuroscientist's Quest for What Makes Us Human*. New York: Norton, 2011. Print.

Savarese, Ralph James and Lisa Zunshine. Interview. "The Critic as Neurocosmopolite; Or, What Cognitive Approaches to Literature Can Learn from Disability Studies." *Narrative* 22.1 (2014): 17–44. Print.

Zunshine, Lisa. *Why We Read Fiction: Theory of Mind and the Novel*. Columbus: Ohio State University Press, 2006. Print.

4 The *Serial* Commodity

Rhetoric, Recombination, and Indeterminacy in the Digital Age

Ellen McCracken

The podcast *Serial* took America by storm in fall 2014. Attracting more than five million listeners by week six, it cemented the new narrative genre into popular consciousness not only because of its compelling story but also because of its accessibility. The one-channel communication medium freed eyes from the screen or page, facilitating the narrative's easy insertion into multitasking while people engaged in other activities such as commuting, exercising, or mechanical tasks. It combined the solitary with the communal—the intimacy of crisp digital voices transmitted through buds inside ears also linked listeners to the millions of others who downloaded the weekly installments and experienced drug-like withdrawal when the author took a break for Thanksgiving week. One year later, several weeks overdue, the second *Serial* series began on December 10, and eager listeners quickly spread the word. Now Bowe Bergdahl replaced Adnan Syed as protagonist. In *Serial* 1, a detective story, Barthes' hermeneutic code predominates—the plot raises questions for listeners, and many are frustrated when the ends aren't tied together. In *Serial* 2, the proairetic code is primary—a recounting of actions that lead to other actions where what Bergdahl did is already known. Both podcasts continue to have real-world effects: Syed was granted a new trial in June 2016, an effect Sarah Koenig favors, and Bergdahl's case worsened to court-martial after the first *Serial* episode about him was released, an outcome Koenig and others hoped would not happen.[1]

Although the characters in *Serial* are real, several narrative strategies common in fiction overcode the telling, as also occurs to some degree in traditional news reporting. A good deal of the program's popularity rests on these techniques through which real people become characters in a larger narrative constructed as we listen. The story is a fragmented and reordered collage of previous and new narrative elements that Sarah Koenig, an author/editor/ narrator/character figure, creates with the help of a public radio team. As in a novel, multiple narrative perspectives frame the content. Now, however, the audience materially inserts itself into the telling during and after listening, carrying on the narration in multiple public venues. This new communicative model enabled by Web 2.0 also shapes the story, which is never finalized as a created artifact either diegetically or temporally: on the diegetic level, Koenig tries to create the illusion that she simply can't make a decision about the character Syed's guilt or innocence; and, on the extra-diegetic temporal plane, listeners carry on the investigative level of the narrative for months and years after the series officially ends. The narrative undecidability has proven an especially lucrative strategy for this new communication medium, which rapidly becomes transformed into a commodity. The aura of postmodern indeterminacy—the epistemological position that nothing can be known with certainty—opens the cultural text to a wide variety of consumers, inviting them to participate in the narrative and to construct possibilities for the closed ending that audiences frequently desire. The text becomes a better commodity precisely because more people can find pleasing points of entry through its appearance of non-conclusive openness. This chapter argues, then, that the attractive rhetorical tropes of fiction and postmodern undecidability that *Serial* employs, in conjunction with new forms of Web 2.0 audience participation, and a network of commercial paratexts combine to create a new kind of mass cultural commodity in the digital age.

Audiences in the Age of Forensic Fandom and Spreadability

Serial is a new model of re-combinatory narrative in the digital age. Koenig and team construct a collage, mash-up, repositioning of old documents, and intercalation of new material. As in a film or video, she reframes narrative segments, chooses an order of audio "shots," makes digital cuts and splices, inserts music, and even adds personal commentary. But now the audience also engages in recombination *while* the cultural text is being created and sometimes affects its ongoing construction. Listeners gather other documents, reorder and reprocess the material Koenig presents, and publish these discoveries, assertions, and guesses on the Internet. The *Serial* team sifts through these public postings and inserts some of them into the in-process episodes.[2] While many in the audience function as what Stuart Hall would term "negotiating listeners," accepting some elements of the texts that *Serial* puts before them and rejecting others, and debating about the issues with others online, some become oppositional listeners, rejecting many of the podcast's assertions, and they communicate this to the *Serial* team as the text is unfolding.

Already in the 1960s, Umberto Eco cautioned against the Frankfurt School's unidimensional critique of the mass media as a culture industry that imparted capitalist ideology to the masses via one-way communication.

Similarly, he critiqued Marshall McLuhan, who, in Eco's view, collapsed the distinctions between the channels of communication, the codes the sender employs, the messages sent, and the distinct codes employed by receivers of the messages: "the message becomes what the receiver makes of it, applying to it his own codes of reception, which are neither those of the sender nor those of the scholar of communication" ("Cogito" 235). Further,

> [t]he mass communication universe is full of these discordant inter-pretations: . . . variability of interpretation is the constant law of mass communications. The messages set out from the Source and arrive in distinct sociological situations, where different codes operate.
>
> (Eco, "Towards" 141)

Now, five decades later, the affordances of Web 2.0 give audiences the almost immediate material means through which to leave a public record of their active engagement with a podcast such as *Serial*: their divergent decodings of the messages, their engagement in intra-audience communica-tion, their creation of feedback loops, and their important new role in shap-ing the ongoing message of the sender.

Although the primary text is comprised entirely of digital sound, the serialized story spread beyond its borders to other media as soon as the episodes were transmitted. Besides print, television, and digital journalism about the podcast, audience members extended the plot in many new public forums. Sarah Koenig's primary narrative strategy of dialogic focalization, in which plot is constructed through fragments of interviews with multiple characters, was reenacted in other media and digital formats as listeners joined the polyphony by recording their views and interpretations online, expanding solitary listening to the sites of communal commentary. *Serial* is not a single text but what Henry Jenkins terms a spreadable artifact that is recombined and distributed across several media and digital venues.[3] Jason Mittell's distinction between spreadable and "drillable" fandom is also at work on *Serial*, with the two functioning as "different but complementary vectors" (290). Thousands of fans engage in forensic "drilling," in which they go deeper and deeper into the evidence, the facts presented, and the inconsistencies, posting this work online as active participants in the nar-rative. Similarly, audience members upload parodies and analytical videos on YouTube and other social media to create their own narratives about the podcast and its content. Celebrating postmodern indeterminacy, Koe-nig's intervention is popular adjudication that is never finalized. Beginning to "retry" Adnan Syed on the digital podcast inspires listeners to partici-pate in the narrative themselves online by engaging in unconcluded "jury" deliberations. Koenig hasn't interviewed *them*, and they insist that they have something important to say. Their digital interventions crowdsource the new people's trial that Koenig instigates with her innovative model of serialized storytelling in the digital age.

Postmodern Doubt and the Illusion of "People's Power"

But what if the veneer of postmodern indeterminacy is only a façade? What if Koenig's pretense of objectivity is only that—a mediating shell that attempts to hide (beneath the protocols of objective, investigative journalism) her strong personal opinion that Syed should not have been convicted? The narratalogical and discursive levels of the podcast show how this strategy functions. The podcast is one among three levels of power that underlie society's efforts to engage in popular, democratic, and fair decisions about guilt and punishment of crimes. All three levels engage in re-combinatory strategies: they gather, interpret, and rearrange heterogeneous texts in order to construct narratives that they contend are overlain with truth.

The first level is the judicial system—court proceedings based on police investigations and the strategies of competing lawyers who recombine evidence and oratory to convince jury members of guilt or innocence. Here, despite the frequent efforts of adjudicators to push the limits and break out of the imposed restraints, a strict legal system predominates—the rules of adjudication, punishment, and incarceration. It is the top level of power.

The second level is the fourth estate—here, investigative journalism in the digital age. Koenig retries Syed extrajudicially, scrutinizing and rereading the evidence, adding new material, overlaying her opinion, and creating a re-combinatory mash-up for massive digital consumption as a serialized podcast. The beginnings of an extrajudicial "people's court" are initiated, and the rules of supposedly objective, fair-minded journalism predominate in contrast to those of the legal system. An intermediary level of power obtains as an early stage of what Jenkins terms spreadable media occurs: Koenig and team give voice to some of those who were previously not heard, and allow the millions of listeners to experience in a new light fragments of some of the voices of those who did present evidence.

The third level is the massive user-generated content that arises. Here is a full-fledged example of spreadable media in which thousands of people participate in online forums to present opinions, theories, and their own investigations for anyone else to see. This secondary engagement in digital networking amplifies the many direct conversations people have off-line about Syed's guilt or innocence. Now, digital participants create thousands of visual, verbal, and auditory mash-ups using the evidence Koenig presents and combining it with other sources. They include links to other forums and information that allow viewers to embark on seemingly endless navigational paths to additional information and opinions. For example, a commentator with the screen name *Surrerialism* creates a word cloud of Jay's February 28, 1999, police interview, posting it on a *Serial* Reddit on January 1, 2015.[4] This visualization functions as an initial metatext, offering viewers a different view of what they have listened to on the podcast. Words such as "ah," "um," "like," and "yeah" have the highest frequency and loom large in the word cloud, along with "know," "car," "back," and "gonna." Seeing such a quantitative and visual representation of the large numbers of fillers, hesitations, and colloquialisms in Jay's discourse might affect people's reinterpretation of the recordings they hear of the statements he gives to the police.

This third level departs the furthest from the rules and constraints of judicial proceedings, evidence, and the law, and, to a certain degree, it is primarily an illusion of people's power.[5] Paradoxically, the larger the number of people involved in this recombination of evidence and interpretation, the less power the discourse has. Over a year after the podcast and the massive popular commentary, Syed's case was sent back to a lower court where in February 2016 he had a post-conviction hearing for an appeal to introduce additional evidence. Even though on June 30, 2016, Syed was granted a new trial, showing the important role of investigative journalism and its new dissemination through podcasts, slow, careful legal rulings still hold the ultimate power. In August, Maryland prosecutors appealed the June ruling, further drawing out the process.

Despite the legal system ultimately prevailing, the audience *does* engage in powerful modes of textual production. It participates in the construction of the podcast by active listenership, by discussing the case in online forums and with friends, and by restructuring the narrative segments Koenig presents. Listeners have an active hand in creating the characters, especially the protagonist Syed, whose self-narration through dialogic interaction with Koenig they scrutinize, evaluate, and reshape. The perceived firsthand engagement with his voice through the crisp digital sound evokes a sense of reliability through which listeners can form their own opinions about his guilt or innocence. They interpret and parse his speech, together with the utterances of the other characters, including those of the principal narrator, Koenig. Some of these micro-participatory strategies of the audience are in turn integrated into the ongoing production of the podcast, changing its trajectory and remaking the text with this permanent, searchable record of the active listenership. Koenig notes, for example, that Bergdahl's friend Kim Harrison contacted the program after listening to it and that interviews with her were then introduced into subsequent episodes.[6]

The Pleasure and Rhetoric of the Constructed Narrative

Even with this strong audience role of transformation of the sender's text, the relative power of the podcast itself invites narratalogical and rhetorical analysis to understand its immense popular attraction as a twenty-first-century cultural artifact. Like the chapters of a novel, its episodes can be experienced sequentially in weekly intervals as a series of discrete but connected units, or in the binge mode—the addictive form of listening made possible by archived files on the Internet. The podcast is a story with many sub-stories and narrative tributaries, and it allows listeners to try on different perspectives on the crime. It is characterized by a surfeit of information with a large quantity of details that are difficult to process and retain. Unlike real-time broadcast television or radio, *Serial*'s segments can be stopped, re-listened to, and reexamined. The utterances live on in cyberspace to be reheard and studied if people desire.

Koenig creates a strong, attractive persona both in the podcast and outside it in interviews and public appearances. In contrast to print narrative, where the voice(s) of the implied author and/or narrator are not aurally experienced, in *Serial* we hear the author telling us the story directly, as in oral narrative traditions. Her pleasing digitized voice draws us in with its intimate style of telling. Colloquialisms, slang, "cool" words, and lilting intonation characterize her auditory performance. Almost intimately, as we listen through earbuds, she appears to be directly speaking to us individually with the utmost honesty, good intentions, and fairness to both sides of the guilt/innocence question. Her striking performance in dramatically reading the carefully crafted written text is a major element of its power. Bringing her undergraduate training in drama to this vocal performance, she widely attracts listeners despite the usually more exciting visual media that predominate in our age. We return each week to experience the repeated, familiar nuances of her voice, eager also to hear the new elements of content in her ongoing detective trail.

The link between repetition and novelty in serials that Eco ("Interpreting Serials") analyzes, extends beyond Sarah's voice to the familiar paratexts of overlain music, ads, and previews that we look forward to.[7] We become fond of these repeated tropes along with the voices of the interviewed characters. We desire these familiar textual markers just as we hunger for novelty, awaiting new plot information every week. The theme song, the musical transitions between segments, the exciting voices of Sarah and the other characters, and even the ads and previews at the beginning and end of episodes form a network of comfort and stability week after week. But we also desire novelty—new information, new voices, and new plot details that must accompany the familiar repeated tropes.

Our pleasure is also enhanced by delay, as Dennis Porter argues is central in detective fiction, as we wait over the twelve weeks, hoping for an outcome and resolution. Even when listening in the binge mode, there are inevitable delays in consuming the podcast straight through without interruption. Some binge listeners even try to stretch out the last episodes, experiencing a foretaste of nostalgia because the narrative pleasure will soon end. Koenig herself points out that, in this new form of journalism, added levels of artifice and artistry draw people in. "Truthful reporting can be artistic," she notes, and this is precisely what creates empathy, interest, and audience engagement. "When people listened," she argues, "the same part of their brain reacted as when they watch [shows] such as *House of Cards* or *Breaking Bad*" (Koenig and Snyder).[8] The traditional rules of professional investigative journalism and judicial proceedings limit such artistic embellishments when reporting events or conducting official court cases. But, here, it is one of the distinct rhetorical strategies of this new kind of lengthy serialized reporting.[9]

How does the narrative construction of *Serial* compel listeners to eagerly await and consume the episodes? Emplotment is central to readers' desire. While we know that Syed was convicted of murdering his ex-girlfriend in high school, we don't know the details of *how* the murder and the guilty verdict happened. Desire for an accounting of these details impels the narrative forward. As Eco notes with respect to the strategy of suspense in the *Superman* series, unpredictability is central. For listeners of *Serial*, like readers of the *Superman* comic, in a very real sense, the events can be said *not* to have happened narratively before the podcast tells this story; they happen unpredictably for the audience *while* it is being told. The emplotment of Syed and Bergdahl and their transformation into characters occur for listeners at the level of discourse. The story that Sarah and the podcast team construct overcodes the narrative events of the murder, the investigation of the crime, and the trial and imprisonment of Syed. This outer narrative is the reinvestigation and retelling of the inner narrative. Most listeners only know the events of the inner narrative through their arrangement and retelling in the outer narrative that Koenig constructs. Discourse, in effect, *creates* the events.

Koenig constructs fictions—possibilities of what happened—all undergirded by her overarching perspective. Part of the podcast's power is the direct dialogism to which we are witness. Many of the recorded voices of the characters directly address Sarah as interlocutor, telling their stories in first person. In her role as frame narrator, Sarah also reports others' narratives both directly and at various removes. She pretends to employ third-person, objective, fly-on-the-wall narration; her profession as an experienced reporter requires that she be neutral and unbiased, an uninvolved onlooker who is not essential to the plot. But Sarah's perspective has profound effects on both the inner and the outer narratives. As we listen to her narration and her dialogues with the people whom the podcast turns into characters, we forget the rhetorical and digital mediations, temporarily feeling that we are listening directly to Sarah and her interlocutors. Paying attention to the events in the unfolding narrative segments, we often forget the podcast's rhetorical strategies, but they are crucial to making the raw material of the inner narrative pleasurable.

Koenig and the production team create a narrative about the previous narrative of the murder, its investigation, and the judicial proceedings. The new *Serial* narrative employs layers of compound focalization to cast the original characters in the new story (see Figure 1).

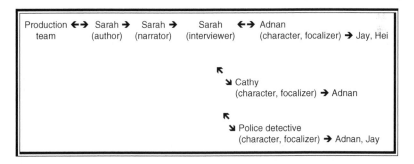

Figure 1

Dialogic interaction (◀▶) underlies both the production and the telling of the narrative. Many characters are themselves focalizers (➜) of other characters. We are invited to look through the eyes of the character speaking as focalizer of the other characters and events in the inner story. We can compare their voices to point-of-view, over-the-shoulder shots in film. The pseudonymous "Cathy" in Episode 6, for example, whose recorded voice is distorted for anonymity, tells us how bad Adnan looked the evening after the crime, stoned and slumped on pillows on her living room floor. Seeming desperate, he asked someone who called his cell phone: "Well, what am I going to do? What am I going to say? [The police are] going to come talk to me!" And then he left abruptly. Cathy narrates the events through her point of view that Adnan's behavior was extremely strange. Sarah directly addresses her, reports in third-person segments some of what Cathy recounts, and interjects her own valorizations of the narrative sequence at the end. In this double encoding, Sarah's focalization overlays that of Cathy—the place where Koenig chooses to insert Cathy's voice in the larger narrative, the questions Sarah asks, her tone of voice, and her commentary. Sarah focalizes Cathy focalizing Adnan.

Sarah is a character in the audio narrative that we listen to at the same time that she is the author of the written text she performs. She functions as author, narrator, interviewer, and character. Over the weeks of the podcast, Sarah the character develops as she performs and comments on her learning process and as she models for us the semi-objective investigative paths she wishes us to follow. She invites us to empathize with her struggle to ascertain the truth, and to participate in this effort with her. In the case of Syed, her multiple narrative roles invite us to agree that, despite his conviction, reasonable doubt surrounds his guilt; and, in the Bergdahl case, she urges us to follow the conclusions that she is more open about this time—that he has already been punished enough for his desertion.

In *Serial* 2, Koenig is unable to have any direct dialogic interaction with the protagonist. The additional mediation of the filmmaker Mark Boal adds a layer of focalization to the narrativization of the protagonist Bergdahl. We hear Boal's voice and experience his thoughts, and he becomes another character in the outer narrative. Boal is an additional major focalizing character since his dialogic interventions have so strongly shaped the raw material from which Koenig must work. The compound focalization in *Serial* 2 employs an additional level of mediation (see Figure 2).

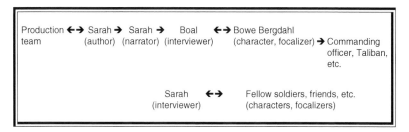

Figure 2

Koenig first invites us to be jurors to weigh the case with her, and then she urges us to agree with her that the truth about Adnan's guilt is unknowable. But many listeners revolt, insisting on their cognitive acumen and detection skills. Although she invokes undecidability as the overarching frame of the narrative, inviting listeners to languish in the impossibility of constructing a truthful version of the 1999 events, her overarching "hand-of-God" desires to narratively transform Syed from definitively guilty to the opposite—*not* definitively guilty beyond a reasonable doubt. She engages in the primary narrative strategy that Todorov terms mythological, in which transformation occurs by negation, "the passage from A to non-A" (30). Although the narrating voice in *Serial* represents itself and the issue of Syed's guilt as undecideable, in fact it strongly invites us to construct a narrative of negation in which Syed should not have been convicted. Even if Koenig ostensibly leaves listeners with non-closure and indefiniteness, they re-narrativize *Serial* while they are listening and commenting, attempting to construct alternative narratives to make sense of the material presented, to have their say in these extrajudicial proceedings.

For example, some Reddit contributors argue that Adnan's claim to not remember anything about that momentous day is suspect. Liars often deliberately provide few details in their stories so that they will not become caught in contradictions, the Redditors note. Another critical *New York Times* reader points to several flaws in the Syed case:

> While Koenig flapped and floundered all over the place in her emotionalism and undisciplined ramblings, [Dana] Chivvis . . . focused on logic. Koenig ran on and on about Adnan's good looks and big brown "doe" eyes. She repeatedly skitted away from crucial facts such as (1) the red fiber found under Hae's head coupled with Jay's allegation that Adnan wore red gloves the day of the murder, (2) the existence of non-Hae skin cells under Hae's fingernails, w/h were never tested for DNA, coupled with the fact—something Koenig omits completely—that the State could've gotten a search warrant for Adnan's & Jay's DNA in 1999, & of course Mr. Protesting-My-Innocence Adnan could've consented to give them his DNA, & (3) Adnan's repeated requests, despite his 15-year-long protest of innocence, that his original trial attorney plead him out (the whole basis for his current appeal).
>
> (Garner, comment by *Aldkg*)

Dissatisfied with Koenig's strategy of non-closure, listeners engage in oppositional interpretations and insist on delineating definitive conclusions. They do not want Hae's murder to become the "perfect crime"—an unsolved one; when Koenig admits her inability to "solve" the crime, the criminal wins.

Another key rhetorical strategy Koenig frequently employs is to admit things that "look bad" for Adnan, only to quickly create doubt about their reliability for proving his guilt. In this sense, the entirety of Episode 6 with the interview of Cathy discussed above is what Barthes terms "inoculation," a strategy through which an advertisement admits a product's shortcoming only to bury that admission under a slew of praise, inoculating us against any concern we might have about the shortcoming. Koenig tells us directly at the beginning of Episode 6 that she will now lay out together all of her findings that point to Adnan's culpability—in effect, to get them out of the way.

The interviewed characters are imperfect witnesses who cannot see events in their entirety. They are not objective narrators, nor do they share their thoughts fully. As we eavesdrop, they often appear to speak directly to us, but we know that they are first-person limited narrators and we wonder about their veracity, either on our own or with Koenig's prompting. We constantly waver between viewing them as reliable or unreliable narrators, and sometimes as both, as occurs, for example, when Koenig points out inconsistencies such as Jay's various contradictory versions of events told to the police. The voices of both protagonists—Syed and Bergdahl—and those of many other characters are overlain with the autobiographical simulacrum—that is, the appearance of truth when telling one's own story. John Paul Eakin points to the slipperiness of "truth" in all autobiography, but here—because of the characters' current or potential status as criminals, truthful or falsifying witnesses, and biased friends—they evoke more suspicion in listeners than do others who employ autobiographical discourse. Additionally, Koenig's careful manipulation of editing, collage, comments, intonation, and other performative levels urges us to balance suspicion with sympathy.

Serial takes strong positions beneath the veneer of postmodern uncertainty. Koenig emphasizes her position at the end of Episode 1 with music playing in the background: "I talk to Adnan regularly and he just doesn't *seem* like a murderer" (48:21). Later, in a serious, confessional tone, she sternly warns, "But I *have* to tell you *this*: Adnan also asked [Hae] for a ride after school that day" (Episode 6), revealing her point of view that she would rather not have to tell us this. Even more clearly in the last episode, she shows her hand, directly stating that in her view Syed was not legally proven guilty. In *Serial* 2, she comments: "To me, more than anything, this moment in the mountain fortress [when he escaped out of the window] puts all talk about Bowe being a Taliban sympathizer to rest. . . . When I finally heard Bowe talk about his time with the Taliban, I thought, no, he does not sound like a traitor!" (Episode 3). Although she asks Adnan why there is no record of his trying to phone Hae on his new cell phone in the days after her disappearance (strongly suggesting that he knew she would not answer because she was dead, not just missing), Koenig backs off with only a sigh—"Oh, . . ."—when he gives the hard-to-believe excuse that he was hearing news about the search for Hae from fellow students. Many listeners are frustrated when after all these weeks of telling us the story, Koenig does not reveal a definitive finding that her investigation has uncovered. She floats in the middle, noting that there was not enough evidence to convict him in court but that she is not entirely convinced of his innocence either.

Behind the narrative strategy of recombination, the discursive reordering of the events of the stories, this journalist's perspective is strong. She arranges, reframes, collates, cuts, interrupts, expresses doubts and judgments, and performs. In the manner of ancient oral storytelling, Koenig "holds the speaker's staff," her top-of-the-line microphone, as we addictively listen on our digital devices. The underlying structural homologies in the episodes of this narrative are visible in multiple rhetorical strategies, including the arrangement and telling, the creation of a sense of doubt and deliberation, of looking at both sides, of continual questioning, and of introducing ostensible culpability, then countering or overlaying it with doubt. As this narrative spreads to social media and the Internet, thousands of listeners challenge the façade of postmodern uncertainty, expressing their certainty in the digital people's court. And, in this process, *Serial* unexpectedly becomes a lucrative media commodity.

The Paratexts of *Serial* and Its Commodification

While few today insist that mass communication simply imparts ideology from the culture industry as the Frankfurt School argued, it is still important to call attention to the commercial nexus of *Serial*. Eco has argued that the media appear merely "to act as thermometer, reporting a rise in temperature," while in fact "they are actually part of the fuel that keeps the furnace going" ("The Sacred" 91). As we have seen, both *Serial* 1 and 2 have extended their narratives by fueling new judicial proceedings for both Syed and Bergdahl— outcomes that Koenig desires in the first case and disapproves of in the second. At the same time, the two seasons of *Serial* have also intensified their own furnaces with respect to their identity as media commodities. The rhetorical narrative overlays, the ostensible aura of undecidability, and the unprecedented active participation of listeners have all catapulted *Serial* into commercialism—a burgeoning moneymaking enterprise.

Here, analysis of the commercial paratexts of *Serial* is revelatory. Gérard Genette's seminal study of the crucial role of paratexts in shaping the meaning of print literary texts draws us to examine the micro-texts surrounding the main text of *Serial*, such as the overlain musical themes, the titles of the episodes, the advertising blurbs inserted in the episodes, the program's website, its Twitter and Facebook feeds, the commentary and visual material that listeners post on the Internet, and Koenig's personal commercial ventures related to the program. This immense network of paratexts merits its own dedicated study, but here I will focus on two examples of paratexts that directly affect the commercialization of the podcast: one, the indirect and direct advertising messages overlain on the episodes as peritexts, and, two, an important delayed authorial epitext that Koenig constructs with producer Julie Snyder outside the podcast as a huge money-making enterprise to capitalize on the program's popularity.[10]

From the start, the experimental program needed to attract sponsorship and funding, and it employed several rhetorical practices of the culture industry to sustain itself. Each episode was framed at the beginning and end by short public radio blurbs for sponsors, such as "Brought to you by . . . MailChimp." The podcast producer Dana Chivvis "voxed" this first sponsor's ad by randomly recording people on the street who agreed to "voice" the name of the sponsoring company for the podcast, and she created a collage of these recordings in the studio. A tourist learning English struggled to pronounce the company's name, humorously guessing, "Mail Kimp?" This then became viral along with the podcast. Although MailChimp signed up for the brief ad based on a projected 300,000 downloads, that figure was reached after only five days, and the program attained five million downloads by week six. By March 2016, *Serial* 1 and 2 had garnered 175 million downloads, and sponsors flocked to purchase brief ads on the program (Koenig and Snyder; Kantrowitz).

While advertising was the only revenue for Season 1, listeners contributed thousands of dollars to help fund Season 2 after Koenig issued an appeal for support during the podcast. As advertisers clamored to buy the short plugs even after the program ended, the producers spliced new ads into the episodes of Season 1 for subsequent listeners. Like watching reruns on TV, in fall 2015 when people downloaded or re-listened to old episodes of Season 1, they heard ads for CVS and the movie *Steve Jobs*, a film that had not been released when the podcast originally streamed. Pandora announced a deal with NPR to stream episodes in real time with somewhat lengthier ads by companies such as Warner Brothers and Esurance. Pandora also superimposed "ad skin" displays on the listener's phone, which, like the audio spot, can be clicked to go to the sponsor's website (Johnson). Koenig then advertised the new Pandora stream of *Serial* in the end credits of the program—for example: "And, special thanks to Pandora where you can now listen to *Serial* Seasons 1 and 2" (Season 2, Episode 2, 56:45).

Koenig's persuasive voice reads the ads in the Season 2 episodes for companies such as Audible.com and Squarespace. But she also engages in a secondary advertising strategy that indirectly leads people to the ads. To keep the audience listening to the commercials at the end, she follows the television industry's model of the delayed preview: "Stay tuned for what's coming up on the next episode of *Serial*. But first . . ." (Season 2, Episode 2). Like the end-of-episode previews in television series, the podcast presents snippets of the characters' voices to be heard in the next episode. Koenig also advertises the *Serial* website, urging readers to view extra material there and sign up for a newsletter: "this week we've got a 3-D map where you can fly over OP Mest, Yosuf Khel, and Fob Sharana. . . . It is very cool!" Statistical documentation of listener response, such as hits on the website and the emails of those who sign up for the newsletter, is crucial to selling more ads for the podcast.

These unpaid program plugs follow the commercial model, but real commercialism underlies the purchased ads that Koenig reads, such as this ten-second one: "Support for *Serial* comes from Audible with more than 180,000 audiobooks. Experience stories that surround you and keep you coming back. Start your 30-day trial with a free audiobook of your choice at audible.com/serial" (Season 2, Episode 1). In this implicitly self-referential spillover, Koenig promotes purchases from Audible.com by subtly promising listeners that they will experience more of the immersive storytelling they are enjoying in her podcast. The audiobook company will be able to track new purchasers who enter its site through the "/serial" link. At the end of the final episode of *Serial* 2, Koenig reads an ad for *This American Life*, the larger NPR program that spawned the *Serial* spinoff.

Koenig and Associate Producer Julie Snyder began a national speaking tour June 6, 2015, that extended into 2016, while they were still creating episodes in the Season 2 podcast. The company All American Speakers lists Koenig's fee as $50,000 and above ("Sarah Koenig Biography"). This delayed authorial epitext gave listeners who could afford the expensive ticket prices the opportunity for embodied, real-time contact with the person behind the addictive crisp digital voice in their earbuds. Great excitement pervaded the large auditorium where I attended, filled with hundreds of youthful listeners who wildly applauded the new media star Koenig. "Binge-Worthy Journalism: Backstage with the Creators of *Serial*" began in the dark with audio clips from the two seasons and an accompanying montage of visuals on the screen. The presentation functioned as a paratextual metacommentary on the podcast through which attendees could learn some of the authorial and editorial strategies that the star and the producer employed to create the digital text. With excerpts from the program playing in the background, the now-embodied voices of Koenig and producer Snyder, amplified in the auditorium, became embedded in the reheard phrases of the podcast that fans recognized, laughed at, and enjoyed again. It was as if the newly formed community of the audience and the creators was commenting on, reinterpreting, reliving, and reminiscing about an enjoyable family vacation.

Readers have always been curious about and fascinated by information about an author's creative processes. Not only did this delayed authorial epitext extend the narrative of the podcast and its pleasure, but it gave some information about the unseen process of production. This heavily commercial performance in effect created another narrative to accompany the podcast, a metanarrative that would reshape the interpretation of the original text. For example, Koenig's tour attempted to reframe the podcast's

authorship as a co-creation, where the presence and commentary of producer Julie Snyder stood in metonymically for the substantial production
team at public radio station WBEZ in Chicago. While the audience was
there primarily to hear and have contact with the star, Snyder's crucial role
in co-creating the podcast tweaked its way into this re-narrativization. For
example, almost as if giving a footnote reference to attribute credit properly,
Koenig notes that one of Snyder's emails gave her the opening for the first
episode: "You're not a detective or a private eye," Snyder cautioned Koenig after reading the draft. Koenig confesses that she "stole" this idea for
the opening segment from Snyder, now retroactively giving the producer
credit. Despite the fact that Koenig *does* function extensively as a detective
throughout the episodes, in hindsight Snyder's advice set the stage for the
postmodern uncertainty of the overall podcast, already opening the possibility that there would be no definitive conclusion. The new paratext created in the speaking tour also gave Snyder credit for *Serial*'s imitation of
television's commercial paratexts such as the initial segments "Previously,
on *Serial* . . .," the concluding "teasers" or previews, the strategy of ending
episodes with cliffhangers, and the weekly recording from Global Tel Link
about the collect call from Syed in prison.

Creative journalism in the digital age becomes an immense profit-making
enterprise that is lucrative not only for the radio network that produces it but
personally for the new media star Koenig. I would argue that the pleasurable rhetorical overlay and the many narrative strategies common in fiction
that the podcast employs distance *Serial* from traditional professional journalism. This new hybrid form of journalism mixed with the attractive tropes
of fiction draws in huge audiences. The media's continual pressure for the
new and innovative in order to increase economic profit (even public radio)
gave birth to this new mode of investigative journalism consumed digitally.
Without doubt, this commercial nexus will shape the journalist's choice of
subjects for new podcasts, and the new star may be ultimately wooed away
by a larger media conglomerate. For continued success, Koenig and team
will have to carefully negotiate the combination of tradition and innovation
that Eco outlined, finding variations on the lucrative rhetorical strategies
and the aura of undecidability that created multiple points of entry for a
wide variety of consumers.

Notes

1. The verdict granting Syed a new trial was appealed in early August by Maryland prosecutors. Within days of the first episode of *Serial* 2 and the massive
   news media coverage it garnered not only about itself but about the Bergdahl
   case, the Army moved to court-martial Bergdahl. Koenig notified listeners of

this update at the beginning of Episode 2, noting that the two-star general in charge of thoroughly reviewing Bergdahl's case had recommended leniency in light of the sergeant's five years already served as a prisoner of the Taliban. Clearly, the podcast and the massive popular media coverage it fomented for the case contributed to higher-ups in the Army deciding that the stronger measure of court-martial was in order.

2. See Pearson for important observations on such interactions between producers and fans.

3. Listeners, for example, made numerous YouTube videos about the podcast. One parody by *michelleinspace*, for example, had 48,000 viewers. See "Serial, Season 2: The Sarah Koenig Story Teaser."

4. See https://www.reddit.com/r/serialpodcast/comments/2r1jet/word_cloud_of_jay_interview_2281999/.

5. Further, in "Binge-Worthy Journalism," Koenig and producer Julie Snyder point to the ethical dimensions of this snowballing discourse, where participants can write anything they want, sometimes violating the privacy of the people involved in the case, yet avoid responsibility for it, an issue also discussed by Haugtvedt and DeMair in this volume.

6. Koenig introduces the newly discovered friend with a rhetorical "tease" and an incipient narrative tributary to draw listeners in: "In very early July of 2009, just a few days after Bowe went missing, a woman named Kim Harrison went to her local police department in Portland, Oregon to report a missing person" (Episode 5, 1:36).

7. These repeated paratexts in fact change for those who listen to the podcast of *Serial* 1 after 2014. New sponsors' ads are now overlain on the beginning and end of the episodes, replacing some of the original text. For example, ads for the Universal Pictures October 2015 film *Steve Jobs* and the marketing platform Percolate reshape later listeners' engagement with the primary text.

8. Koenig's allusion to the cognitive neuroscience aspect of the pleasure that people experience in listening to podcasts has been documented by researchers at UC Berkeley. See Benedict Carey.

9. Newspapers began to imitate the compelling style of *Serial* in an attempt to attract readers and remain financially viable in the digital age. See, for example, the engaging six-part serial "Framed" in the *Los Angeles Times* beginning September 3, 2016, http://www.latimes.com/projects/la-me-framed/#chapter1.

10. Genette divides paratexts into two main categories. Peritexts are those that surround the main text and are materially attached to it, such as the covers, title, author's name, chapter titles, footnotes, and so on. Epitexts affect the text's meaning but are outside it, such as reviews, advertising, and author interviews. Genette terms such interviews "delayed authorial epitexts."

Works Cited

Barthes, Roland. "Operation Margarine." In *Mythologies*. Trans. Annette Lavers. New York: Hill and Wang, 1972. 41–42. Print.

———. *S/Z: An Essay*. Trans. Richard Miller. New York: Hill and Wang, 1975. Print.

Carey, Benedict. "This Is Your Brain on Podcasts." *New York Times*. 28 Apr. 2016. Web.

Eakin, John Paul. *Fictions in Autobiography: Studies in the Art of Self-Invention.* Princeton, NJ: Princeton University Press, 1985. Print.

Eco, Umberto. "Cogito Interruptus." In *Travels in Hyperreality.* Trans. William Weaver. 1967. New York: Harcourt, Brace, Jovanovich: 1986. 221–238. Print.

———. "Interpreting *Serials.*" In *The Limits of Interpretation.* Bloomington: Indiana University Press, 1990. 83–100. Print.

———. "The Sacred Is Not Just a Fashion." In *Travels in Hyperreality.* Trans. William Weaver. 1979. New York: Harcourt, Brace, Jovanovich, 1986. 89–94. Print.

———. "Towards a Semiological Guerrilla Warfare." In *Travels in Hyperreality.* Trans. William Weaver. 1967. New York: Harcourt, Brace, Jovanovich, 1986. 135–144. Print.

"Episode 1: The Alibi." Narr. Sarah Koenig. *Serial: Season One.* NPR, 3 Oct. 2014. Podcast.

"Episode 2: The Golden Chicken." Narr. Sarah Koenig. *Serial Season Two.* NPR, 17 Dec. 2015. Podcast.

"Episode 3: Escaping." Narr. Sarah Koenig. *Serial Season Two.* NPR, 24 Dec. 2014. Podcast.

"Episode 5: Meanwhile in Tampa." Narr. Sarah Koenig. *Serial Season Two.* NPR, 21 Jan. 2016. Podcast.

"Episode 6: The Case against Adnan Syed." Narr. Sarah Koenig. *Serial Season One.* NPR, 30 Oct. 2014. Podcast.

Garner, Dwight. "Serial Podcast Finale: A Desire for Eureka as the Digging Ends." *New York Times.* 19 Dec. 2014.

Genette, Gérard. *Paratexts: Thresholds of Interpretation.* Trans. Jane E. Lewin. Cambridge: Cambridge University Press, 1997. Print.

Goffard, Christopher. "Framed: A Mystery in Six Parts." *Los Angeles Times.* 3 Sept. 2016. Web.

Hall, Stuart. "Encoding,/Decoding." In *Culture, Media, Language: Working Papers in Cultural Studies, 1972–79.* Ed. Stuart Hall, Dorothy Hobson, Andrew Lowe and Paul Willis. London: Hutchinson, 1980. 128–38. Print.

Horkheimer, Max, and Theodor W. Adorno. *Dialectic of Enlightenment.* New York: Herder and Herder, 1972. Print.

Jenkins, Henry, Sam Ford and Joshua Green. *Spreadable Media: Creating Value and Meaning in a Networked Culture.* New York: New York University Press, 2013. Print.

Johnson, Lauren. "*Serial* Is Landing on Pandora with Backing of Big Brand Advertisers." *Advertising Age.* 19 Nov. 2015. Web. 3 Apr. 2016.

Kantrowitz, Alex. "Inside the Business of the *Serial* Podcast: B-to-B Marketer MailChimp Wins Big as Launch Sponsor." *Advertising Age.* 18 Dec. 2014. Web. 3 Apr. 2016.

Koenig, Sarah and Julie Snyder. "Binge-Worthy Journalism: Backstage with the Creators of *Serial.*" Lecture, University of California, Santa Barbara. 3 Mar. 2016.

Mittell, Jason. *Complex TV: The Poetics of Contemporary Television Storytelling.* New York: New York University Press, 2015. Print.

Pearson, Roberta. "Fandom in the Digital Era." *Popular Communication: The International Journal of Media and Culture* 8.1 (Feb. 2010): 84–95. Print.

Porter, Dennis. *The Pursuit of Crime: Art and Ideology in Detective Fiction.* New Haven: Yale University Press, 1981. Print.

"Sarah Koenig Biography." *All American Speakers.* https://www.allamericanspeakers. com/speakers/Sarah-Koenig/392890. Web. 16 April 2016.

"*Serial, Season 2*: The Sarah Koenig Story Teaser." https://www.youtube.com/ watch?v=ZKmGYB0-dqg. Web.

Todorov, Tzvetan. *Genres in Discourse.* Cambridge: Cambridge University Press, 1990. Print.

5　"What We Know"

Convicting Narratives in *NPR*'s *Serial*

Sandra Kumamoto Stanley

In her mesmerizing and groundbreaking podcast *Serial*, Sarah Koenig investigates the 1999 murder of high school student Hae Min Lee and the conviction of Lee's ex-boyfriend, Adnan Syed. A spin-off of the NPR radio program *This American Life*, the podcast *Serial* (Season One), which completed its first airing in fall 2014, became, according to PBS's Judy Woodruff, "an unexpected phenomenon," and, according to the *Wall Street Journal*, the most popular podcast in the world, setting an iTunes record for the most downloaded podcast of the year (Gamerman; Kelly). In May 2015, *Serial* received a Peabody Award, the first podcast to do so. In her final episode, "What We Know," Koenig admits that legally she had reasonable doubt about Syed's guilt, but personally she continues to nurse doubts about his innocence. Rather than adhering to the conventions of the classic detective genre and providing closure for *Serial*'s listeners, Koenig's final podcast episode foregrounds a postmodern epistemological indeterminacy. In fact, Koenig's tentative ending suggests that her narrative has its own kinship with the metaphysical postmodern detective story—a genre that foregrounds "unresolved, ambiguous, ironic, and self-reflexive investigations" (Sweeney 192), often transcending the more positivist view of "who done it" to ask larger questions concerning identity, meaning, and knowledge.

Soon after the conclusion of *Serial*, Terry Gross (of NPR's *Fresh Air*), in turn, interviewed Koenig, and, in their conversation, Koenig discusses the narrative complexities of her investigation, including her relationship with Adnan Syed, with whom she primarily conversed by phone. Ironically, during the airing of the podcast, both the reporter Koenig and the convict Syed became increasingly sensitive to what they could not control: how the listeners would interpret both of their roles and their narratives. At one point, Syed tells Koenig that he has fought hard in the intervening years since Lee's death to transform the perception that others had of him from a monster back to a human being (Episode 11, "Rumor"). And with the growing popularity of the podcast, both Syed and Koenig find that they have become part of the debate, unable to control their own scripts. Viewers wondered: is Syed manipulating Koenig? Is Koenig manipulating the facts? Both admit their vulnerability in the face of public opinion; both of their narratives are judged, questioned, absolved, and/or convicted in a textual field in which the reader/listener becomes the writer/speaker.

Intriguingly, Koenig shares with Gross how she and Syed argued over the best way to access her podcast. Offering to send him a CD, she desires him to listen to the podcast, while he prefers to read the transcripts of the podcast:

> I don't know if part of him doesn't want to hear it, that he'd rather read it on the page. I don't know. We've argued about that, actually. . . . I'm like, "It's meant to be heard." And he's like, "No, I want to see it in its purest form, on paper." And I'm like, "No, no, no. You're missing a ton. You're missing all kinds of nuance that is happening in people's voices." Or he's taking stuff at face value that I say, that I'm like, "No! If you heard the way I say it, you'd hear that it's like in passing or it's like I'm being ironic, or whatever!" And he's just like, "No, YOU don't get it, the real version is on paper!"
>
> ("Interview")

For Syed, the written word is the "purest form," a script that he can better control and verify as the "real version"; while for Koenig the spoken word, with its nuances and irony, is the richer form that allows for the play of meaning. Their "fight" concerning representations of meaning echoes some of the concerns explored in Roland Barthes' play with the relationship between the work and text, and even Jacques Derrida's disruption of speech and writing—oppositions that Derrida ultimately deconstructs. Both Barthes and Derrida challenge stable, logocentric meaning as illusory and perceive texts as radically plural, embodying a process of deferred significance rather than representing stable objects of meaning. Syed, who is hoping for a retrial, wants to capture a narrative in its "purest form," allowing him to reclaim his legal and social innocence; as he states, "I don't want people to think I'm a monster" (Episode 11, "Rumors"). For him, it's important that the relationship between the signifier and signified remain constant, so that he can contain meaning, minimizing the plural and supplementary nature of language. Koenig, however, despite her role as an objective reporter, prefers a more ambiguous narrative that would allow her to slip from the parameters of stable meaning as well as, we might suggest, the social responsibility of helping to either free or convict Syed (is he a victim of the system or, in Syed's words, a monster?). Each has a competing narrative strategy, and the interpretive stakes are high for both, revealing the illusion of the objectivity of the reporter and of the system of justice and its participants, ultimately disrupting all their slippery narratives. *Serial*—from its podcast mode of chronicling its investigation, to its social depictions of the crime and its major characters, to its metaphysical queries concerning identity, knowledge and justice—foregrounds the self-reflexive concept of storytelling not only because the characters, narrator, and audience are all engaged in attempting to decipher the mystery but also because they become aware that the very act of cognition and meaning making is a struggle that may not ultimately lead to a culminating resolution.

Digital Storytelling

As more than one observer has noted, *Serial* provides a unique genre of audio narratology, a contemporary digital reinvention of an ancient mode of oral storytelling. In his *Gutenberg Galaxy: The Making of Typographic Man*, Marshall McLuhan provides one way of seeing this shift from the oral to electronic age; in this foundational work, he posits that the Gutenberg Age supplanted an oral culture and ushered in a print culture, privileging the eye over the voice, the visual over the acoustic. He suggests that this altering of our cognitive order in turn altered our social order. According to McLuhan, this bound linearity of the written form shaped an individualistic and rational psyche, a capitalistic industrial environment with its Taylorized assembly lines, even a competitive nationalistic mindset. The onset of the electronic age—as marked, for instance, by such sound and transmission technology as radio—creates another paradigm shift, but one that recoups the spoken word and human ear, reversing, according to McLuhan, "the entire direction and meaning of literate Western civilization"—now privileging the partial, the experiential, and the global (262). Intriguingly, McLuhan sees the visual space of print culture as "homogenous and uniform" against the acoustic space of the electronic age that he views as "discontinuous" and "dynamic" (McLuhan and McLuhan 33). For our purposes, McLuhan's theory gives us insight into Syed's own thought processes, as Syed holds on to the print culture of the "typographic man."

Although critics such as Raymond Williams have critiqued McLuhan's sweeping generalizations and technological and cultural determinism, others have emphasized the importance of McLuhan's groundbreaking work that helps to delineate the connection of the electronic age to the human imagination and social change, noting the way that he has anticipated postmodern issues focusing upon the virtual spaces of new media. For some scholars in radio studies, such as Tim Crook, McLuhan's ideas have been the basis of thinking of how "sound recording and electronic transmission" have retribalized the electronic age and how audio/radio drama merges the acoustic and visual space—bringing together the mechanical and electronic soundscape with a powerful "visual force in the psychological dimension" (8). Further highlighting the connection between the electronic age and the human subject, Steven Connor has even argued that such a dynamic transformation of a new media soundscape coincides with the reconceptualization of a contemporary subjectivity—reflected in an anti-foundational and fragmented postmodern self.

Whether or not one agrees with the assertions of these sound and media theorists—and certainly these claims have been contested—podcasts such as *Serial* have recouped oral storytelling in a new media age or, as the above critics suggest, retribalized the digital age. Media theorist Neil Verma asserts, "We are living in a golden age of podcasting" (Rajanala). Koenig and her team are able deftly to intertwine the expectations of older print culture with the science of an Internet era. We have a global audience that can download a podcast that they can listen to whenever convenient, and we have a narrator that uses nineteenth-century serialized storytelling through new media technology. And at the heart of *Serial* are not only the story of guilt and innocence, youth and maturity, love and death, but also the story of the transmission of this tale. For as Koenig muses in her Peabody speech, they never expected *Serial* to become such a popular success—after all, it was, as she states, "a ten hour audio documentary about an old murder that I did not solve" ("Peabody"). Why this fascination?

In part, Koenig creates a narrative experience that emphasizes the process of detection with the promise of discovery for her audience. In his book *Theater of the Mind: Imagination, Aesthetics, and American Radio Drama*, Verma suggests that we should use the term "audioposition" rather than "vantage point" to describe the experience of listening to the radio. He explains, "Listeners do not just 'have' a point of audition; they are 'positioned' by audio composition and components of dialogue" (35). The podcast employs a number of repetitious auditory experiences to engage and position its listeners—for instance, the opening theme song cues the audience to anticipate the next series of events; the beginning format then recaps the voices from past episodes, offering the audience a sense of continuity; and the ending format poses cliff-hanger questions, providing a sense of anticipation for the next installment. Verma describes one of the styles related to audiopositions as an "intimate style" that allows the listener to follow a character or set of characters, developing a certain empathy and knowledge based upon that viewpoint. Koenig's conversational, sometimes-tentative voice invites the audience to join in her inquiry as though she is a confidante sharing her information. Koenig and her team create an intimate relationship with her audience, giving the listener the sense that Koenig is engaged in a process of discovery, even as the audience is "detecting" along with her. In addition, *Serial*'s producers are able to merge an acoustic and visual space in their audience's podcast experiences, as listeners not only attend to Koenig but also imagine her narratives in their minds. At the same time that Koenig shapes her narrative, she does not ostensibly impose her monologic view on her audience; rather, she also incorporates other voices—through documents, interviews, and tape recordings—inviting a polyphony of multiple utterances.

In fact, I would argue that although Koenig primarily uses acoustic space, she also intersperses her narrative with written documents—as though promising her audience the possibility of verifying and interpreting key documents, what Syed describes as the "purest form." In fact, she includes some of these documents on her website, allowing listeners to become readers, with the promise that perhaps they can find the elusive "word" that will unlock the mystery. The first episode, "The Alibi," is titled after Asia McClain's letter that offers Syed his alibi for the time the prosecution accuses him of killing Hae Min Lee. In the first episode, Koenig essentially outlines the whole narrative: Lee's death, Jay Wilds's accusation of Syed as the killer, and Syed's conviction. Yet this titular "alibi" that should provide Syed his freedom becomes only one of the multiple means of understanding the sequence of events for the day of Hae's disappearance; the promised resolution becomes another interpretive possibility. In the second episode, "The Breakup," Koenig chronicles Hae and Adnan's love affair and their breakup, what she describes as both a very common "so high school" tale and a Shakespearean mash up—Adnan first playing Romeo to Hae's Juliet, then Othello to Hae's Desdemona; here, she uses Hae's diary as the central document to let the dead victim literally speak from the past. The two lovers' breakup tale constitutes either the ever-so-familiar and innocuous dissolution of a high school romance or the prosecution's rationale for Adnan/Othello killing Hae/Desdemona. In Episode 4, "Inconsistencies," Koenig focuses upon police records and Wilds' varied descriptions of what happened; after all, Wilds' testimonies form the very basis of the prosecution's case against Syed. While Syed simply notes that he cannot really remember the details of January 13, 1999, the day Lee went missing, Wilds offers multiple and often-conflicting details of that very day. In Episode 5, "Route Talk," Koenig and Dana Chivvis, using the prosecution time line and the cell phone call log, try to puzzle out the discrepancies of both Jay's and Adnan's proposed narratives. While Jay's version of events is not supported by the cell phone log, neither is Adnan's, and Koenig and Chivvis' doubts about Adnan's innocence culminate in their examination of the "Nisha call," a cell phone call that seems to incriminate Syed. As they collect police records, call logs, letters, and testimonies in the succeeding episodes, the possible stories seem to proliferate, exceeding the hoped-for promise that a "bound" print culture could contain and reduce these stories to a single monologic narrative. Instead of achieving clarity, Koenig and her team find that documenting the signifiers of the print culture do not lead them either to discovering a transcendental signified or to achieving epistemological certainty.

Individual Memory and Social Storytelling

In her podcast, Koenig begins with a meditation on memory and ends with larger epistemological questions concerning guilt, innocence, and legal justice. Koenig observes that at the center of this story of crime is a narratological battle, for, in her final episode, she notes, "Adnan told me all he wanted was to take the narrative back from the prosecution, just as an exercise. So people could see his case without makeup on, look at it in the eye up close and make their own judgments" (Episode 12, "What We Know"). Syed is fully aware that his case rests largely on dueling narratives, based on the respective group's interpretation of evidence and testimonies. In the midst of their interviews for *Serial*, Syed sends Koenig two graphs, both entitled the "Price of Tea," that ostensibly chart competing prices of tea in two stores. He then asks Koenig if, as a consumer, she would prefer to shop at a store that had consistent pricing or a store whose prices fluctuated. As soon as she responds that she would prefer to shop at a store with consistent pricing, Syed triumphantly reveals that the graphs are identical in their information but diverge in their presentation. Koenig transcribes Syed's observations:

> "I read a book about a prosecutor who said it's not always about innocent or guilty, it's about who can persuade the jury," Adnan said. "And they're not being dishonest—nothing about that graph is dishonest—but it's kind of misleading. It's darker, it's zoomed in, the heading is underlined. Everything about it is misleading, but it's true information.
>
> "When I first came [to prison], I was naïve to the law, to prison life, to a lot of things," he said. "Now that I'm older, I see guys naïve to the law coming in. I use this graph to illustrate it. Probably people here say, 'Oh my god, Syed showed you that damn graph, didn't he?' And I'm like, 'No it proves a point!' It proves a good point. So I'm kinda infamous for those graphs."
>
> ("The Price of Tea")

Using graphs to prove his point that meaning is not fixed, Syed must paradoxically rely upon "true information" or evidence—whether it's concerning the economics of the price of tea or the legalities of the murder of a young woman—that is shaped by presentation and interpretation. Like the commodity "tea," he realizes that he has been packaged and sold in the system, and the attorneys who are most adept at presenting their narratives about the accused are the ones who convince the jurors that their "graph" is the most effective one. Despite his understanding about the important power of narrative presentations, Syed, however, does not have a compelling narrative of his own to challenge the prosecution's narrative for the key date for his case—January 13, 1999—for he cannot remember the details of what he did on the day of Lee's disappearance.

From the beginning, Koenig realizes that memory is a pivotal part of her story. She spends the opening segment of the first episode contemplating the difficulty of accurately remembering the past. Rather than beginning with a tough interrogation of the characters in the case, she establishes her intimate style by casually asking her nephew Sam and other teenagers if they remember what they were doing six weeks earlier. She concludes that it is difficult to remember a day in the past, unless something significant happened during that day. Koenig realizes that she will be not only relying on the memory of witnesses surrounding the case but also asking individuals to remember events that may have occurred fifteen years previously. At one point, she seems to indicate that memory will solve this case, as she declares that the whole case seemed to be "teetering on her [Asia McClain's] memories of that afternoon" (Episode 1, "The Alibi), but, at another point, she realizes that the convicted Syed cannot remember the details of that day; he cannot construct a counter-narrative that might save him. While Jay's testimony relies upon his ever-shifting narratives and a proliferation of conflicting details, shaped by either his faulty memory or his puzzling fabrications, Syed's testimony is simply based on absence of details. In his interview with Koenig, Syed explains:

> I mean, I do kind of understand that it comes across as—I don't know if it does or doesn't. But it seems like I remember things that are beneficial to me, but things that aren't beneficial to me I can't remember. It's just that I don't really know what to say beyond the fact that a lot of the day that I do remember, it's bits and pieces that come from what other people have said that they remember, right? And it kind of jogs my memory. . . . I mean, the only thing I can say is, man, it was just a normal day to me. There was absolutely nothing abnormal about that day.

Koenig realizes that Syed's vague memory places him in a double bind:

> Adnan knows better than anyone how unhelpful this all is, how problematic. Because it plays both ways. If he's innocent, right, it's any other day. Of course he doesn't remember. But you also read it as, how

convenient. He doesn't remember the day. So no one can fact check him, or poke holes in his story. Because he has no story.

(Episode 1, "The Alibi")

Syed's assertion that the day was normal—not significant—is troubling, for this was the day that Lee disappeared: wouldn't this day simply be significant since on that day he was first alerted by the police that his friend was missing? However, as Koenig suggests, this loss of memory could also be the marker of his innocence, for an innocent person does not prepare an alibi ahead of time. Yet while Wilds presents a detailed, but flawed, narrative that can be checked, Syed's story is unverifiable, for, as Koenig notes, "he has no story." In part, Syed's and Wilds's memories constitute their own narratives of the self, even if, in the case of Syed, it is not to have a narrative—to have "no story." Yet, we know, such concepts as past, present, and memory are complicated issues, especially once that memory comes under scrutiny. As Henri Bergson suggests, the past is not monolithic but consists of multiple layers, each shifting in relationship to the present:

> The present is represented as a plane, with a cone of layers balanced on its point on that plane. The cone represents layers of the past supporting the present. The way to access these levels of past from the present is through memory and/or duration. Memory relates between all these levels of past, performing the operations of selectivity and interpretation for each layer of past.
>
> (156)

Bergson suggests that memory is not uniform and that the mental present and past may continually shift as that past acquires meaning and is reorganized and interpreted in service to selective goals, whether those goals may be motivated by Syed's desire to assert his innocence or Wilds' desire to establish Syed's guilt. The individual is perpetually reclassifying events of the past, present, and future, experiencing that metaphoric "flow of time." As the various characters grapple with the past events, the characters and audience are inevitably forced to think about the very process of memory and how we construct narratives in order to define ourselves.

Of course, Koenig's statement that Syed "has no story" concerning that fateful day in 1999 is an overstatement, for Syed actually suggests that he is remembering the day through a collective framework as others—his parents, his friends, and especially Asia—offer him possible ways to recoup that memory. One could certainly argue that the typical view of memory—which posits the recollection of an individual mind—privileges the individual over the social in the process of reconstructing a past. Yet collective memory and social storytelling are also key factors in the construction of *Serial*'s narratives. When Syed explains his thoughts behind the "Price of Tea" graphs to Koenig, he states that while "nothing about that graph is dishonest," it is "misleading": "It's darker, it's zoomed in, the heading is underlined. Everything about it is misleading, but it's true information." Syed, of course, is also talking about the prosecution's story—how both his personal and his cultural narratives are appropriated and manipulated by the policing and prosecutorial agencies. Drawing from racialized stereotypes, they have "zoomed in" and "underlined" a depiction of a "darker" side—constructing a psychological, social, and cultural narrative of him both as a brooding, enraged ex-lover and as a Muslim of Pakistani origin who would kill Hae to avenge his honor. Syed is depicted no longer as an American teenager testing parental authority but as an Orientalized image of exoticized danger.

Inevitably, the questions of guilt and innocence cannot be separated from the "already said" social discourse. Clearly, gender, ethnic, and racial representations are manipulated by the multiple participants in *Serial*—from the key witnesses in the case, to the legal system, to the narrator and listeners of the podcast. Both the murder victim and her convicted ex-boyfriend are minority teenagers; Lee was Korean American, while Syed is Pakistani American. Moreover, the key prosecution witness against Syed was Jay Wilds (an African American young man and Syed's former friend and drug dealer), and all their stories are being told and interpreted through the point of view of a white reporter. How is each of their stories being shaped and filtered through already existing cultural narratives? A number of critics and listeners of the podcast have critiqued the racial and ethnic representations in this story, asking if the reporter Koenig viewed this murder mystery through the lens of white privilege. Julia Wong, for instance, has critiqued *Serial*'s ideologically charged use of racial tropes. She has asked if Lee and Syed, students in Woodlawn High School's magnet program, are being depicted as "model minorities" against Jay Wilds's portrayal as a "stereotypical black urban youth," acting as the "'thuggish' black foil." Others wondered, along with Koenig, if the makeup of the predominantly black jury affected the verdict. Moreover, is the Muslim Syed, who continues to maintain his innocence and is appealing his case, currently being viewed through the biases of a post-9/11 world (Basu, Cruz, Friedersdorf, and Kilkenny)?

When Koenig asks Shamin Rahman, Adnan's mother, why she believes her son (whom she unwaveringly has perceived as innocent) was ultimately convicted, she quickly replies: discrimination. "It was easy for them to take him"—a "Muslim child" (Episode 10, "The Best Defense"). Although Koenig resists charging the system with institutionalized racism, she understands Shamin's perspective as Adnan's mother shares her feelings of outrage when she first heard the basis of the prosecutor's argument to deny Adnan bail. On the day of the bail hearing, the court was filled with members from Adnan's mosque, the Islamic Society of Baltimore. While Syed's defense lawyer references the Islamic community as part of Adnan's extended family—doctors, lawyers, teachers, and religious leaders who vow to supervise him and accompany him to court—the prosecutor, Vicki Walsh, describes the same community leaders as "aiders and abettors" who would help Adnan to "run away to Pakistan." Walsh then asserts that "there is a pattern . . . where young Pakistani males have been jilted, have committed murder, and have fled to Pakistan" ("The Best Defense"). When her assertions are challenged and proven to be not only misleading but also false, Walsh ultimately writes a letter apologizing to the court. Koenig, however, acknowledges that Walsh's comments only serve as a prelude to the trial, for the social discourse of anti-Muslim preconceptions will permeate the entire trial, including the prosecution's arguments, the witnesses' comments, and even the jurors' perceptions. Koenig wryly notes that the fact that Syed's lawyer, Cristina Gutierrez, spends an extensive (or, in Koenig's words, "nutty") amount of time in her opening statement emphasizing her client's American citizenship demonstrates her concern that "the jurors might be prone to anti-Muslim, anti-foreigner sentiment" (Episode 10, "The Best Defense").

Against the proliferation of discursive social stories, it is no wonder that Syed feels manipulated by the vying perceptions of his case and by prosecutors who have manipulated the social discourses of what Koenig terms "casual prejudice" (Episode 10, "The Best Defense"). In the intervening years since his imprisonment, Syed has become ever more reliant upon the world of facts and ever more suspicious of the world of interpretation. Koenig shares, "Adnan says his biggest fear is not being believed. When he's sure about something, he has a tendency to over explain, to inundate you with facts and information, and corroboration for the facts and information. He doesn't like this tendency in himself, but he says he can't help it" (Episode 6, "The Case against Adnan Syed"). Even as he is challenging the legal-system interpretation of his case, Syed must rely upon the language of that very system—printed words and documentation. He emphatically states to a puzzled Koenig that he does not want to listen to the podcast but desires, instead, "to see it in its purest form, on paper." Adnan demands the documentation of the Age of Gutenberg—texts that appear linear, rational, and verifiable—even though he knows that this flawed system convicted him in the first place; however, he is dependent on that very system to free him, to somehow justify him, to reconstruct his forever-marked identity. As Koenig relays to the listener, all Adnan wants to do is to take the narrative back from the prosecution. No matter what the individual listener's stance may be on Syed's guilt or innocence, most of the podcast's listening public can agree that *Serial* has "taken back" the prosecution's narrative.

The Audience and Storytelling

In her work *Listening Publics*, Kate Lacey has noted that "listening bridges *both* the sensory, embodied experience *and* the political realm of debate and deliberation" (5). Although podcast addressees may listen individually or even provisionally—picking up a half hour here or there—they are also listening as a collective, virtual or actual. Each individual member is listening with a shared public, specifically with an NPR audience. But one may argue that it is really the "political realm and deliberation" that engages the listening public. Intriguingly, Koenig divides *Serial* into twelve episodes, echoing the genre of the epic, and, like the epic, the *Serial* podcast is also embedded in a social and national story.

Serial's listeners carried on the "debate and deliberation" that surround the issues that the show has raised. Sites such as Reddit host discussions and archive materials about the podcast. The listening public insist upon making their own judgments, and, precisely because of the ambiguity of the case (Asia McClain's testimony; the Nisha call; Jay's erratic testimonies; Cristina Gutierrez's once stellar, then tarnished reputation; and the prosecution's unverifiable timeline), that debate erupted and continues to erupt in social media. As they are "listening out" (attentive and anticipatory) and "listening in" (receptive and mediatized), the public engage in a political discourse concerning not only Syed's guilt or innocence but also the very fabric of our social and legal systems (Lacey 4).

Because of Koenig's process-oriented approach and unresolved ending, her audience has especially felt that they, too, could investigate this material. Their passionate debates about Syed's innocence or guilt, the justice system, and the ethical role of the podcast itself speak to the way that media scholars such as Douglas Kellner have contended that new media and the Internet may ideally provide the possibility for a democratic postmodern public sphere "in which people can construct and experiment with identity, culture, and social practices" and engage in informed debates, at the same time recognizing how that very public sphere may be "co-opted by hegemonic forces" (Kahn and Kellner 1–2). As such, the multiple voices and narratives that inhabit the original podcast have now proliferated into a polyphony of narratives, as the listeners become readers and speakers. Moreover, since Syed's own story of legal appeals is ongoing, *Serial*'s audience may choose to continue the podcast through a variety of digital means—whether following Adnan's appeals process, listening to interviews by other participants, or continuing with commenting on discussion sites. As such, the narratives that surround the podcast continue to proliferate beyond the confines of the twelve episodes.

In fact, the producers have included three updated podcasts, approximately fifteen minutes each, on the *Serial* (Season One) website, in which Koenig attends Syed's February 2016 hearing for a new trial and reports what she witnesses. At this point in the appeal process—specifically Syed's petition for post-conviction relief—Syed's lawyer, Justin Brown, is essentially focusing upon putting elements of the trial on trial. Key in his argument is that Syed's original lawyer, Cristina Gutierrez, provided ineffective counsel, for she did not interview and utilize an important alibi witness, Asia McClain. In addition, Brown asserts that the prosecutors did not inform the jurors that information concerning cell towers and incoming calls could be unreliable; hence, jurors could have been relying upon misleading data. In a series of taped telephone conversations, Koenig discusses with producer Dana Chivvis the highlights of the hearing. In this dialogic exchange, Koenig shares her observations, and Chivvis (positioning herself as the audience) asks questions, seeks clarification, and offers her opinions. In their exchange, they alternate from suggesting that the evidence from the defense's appeal sounds "inconclusive" to "convincing" ("Hearing," Day Three). Koenig also recognizes the meta-discursive nature of the hearing, as she comments, "*Serial* was part of her [Asia McClain's] testimony" ("Hearing," Day One). In her own report on the hearing for NPR, Andrea Seabrook wryly remarks, "It's like a crazy meta-feedback loop where journalists dig up witnesses and evidence which are then used in the court proceedings which are then covered by journalists."

Of course, when Syed was first convicted, the Lee family, in contrast to Syed's family and many *Serial* listeners, had reached their own closure. However, *Serial* and Adnan's appeals process inevitably disrupt their perceived "sense of an ending" (Kermode). At the hearing, Lee's family asks Deputy Attorney General Thiru Vignarajah to read their statement, addressing those who would challenge the original trial's narrative of guilt and punishment. Suffering from "reopened wounds," the family writes: "It remains hard to see so many run to defend someone who committed a horrible crime, who destroyed our family, who refuses to accept responsibility, when so few are willing to speak up for Hae. She stood up for what was right, regardless of popular opinion. Unlike those who learn about this case on the internet, we sat and watched every day of both trials—so many witnesses, so much evidence." They wish to "bring this chapter to an end" (Miller). However, Syed's supporters interpret the Lee family's statement as influenced and shaped by a hegemonic State that wishes to silence their alternate views. Both are fighting to ensure their own respective denouements.

At the end of Episode 11, Syed sends Koenig a letter in which he observes,

> As I look back now . . . I realize there was only three things I wanted after I was convicted. To stay close to my family, prove my innocence and to be seen as a person again. Not a monster.

Syed asserts that he "was able to find the peace of mind in prison" that he had lost at his trial, for "guards, inmates, staff, people . . . [who] see me everyday, recognize me as someone whose word can be trusted." He then writes, "It doesn't matter to me how your story portrays me, guilty or innocent, I just want it to be over" (Episode 11, "Rumors"). At this point, Syed expresses his exhaustion, for, in participating in the *Serial* podcast, he has essentially become a text that has been analyzed and interpreted and co-opted. Previously, he had at least felt that he owned his words, for, as he notes, others recognized him "as someone whose word can be trusted," who provided them with a "real version," a verifiable narrative of himself. But the *Serial* podcast disrupts his "peace of mind," as he transforms from a speaker to a text, feeling his own sense of himself as a coherent, unified agent being undermined.

While Syed wishes for the podcast to come to an end, Koenig is also searching for her own narrative closure. In the final episode, Syed asks her if she has an ending. She states, "Of course I have an ending. We're going to come to an ending today" (Episode 12, "What We Know"). Here, Koenig elides ending as a product with ending as a process. In fact, her irresolute resolution reflects that tension. When she started, Koenig assumed that "certainty, one way or the other[,] seemed so attainable. We just needed to get the right documents, spend enough time, talk to the right people, find his alibi." However, the documents, evidence, and facts do not provide a coherent certainty; they provide only a postmodern indeterminacy. In the end, Syed warns Koenig that she will never reach epistemological closure: "I don't think you'll ever have one hundred percent or any type of certainty about it. The only person in the whole world who can have that is me. For what it's worth, whoever did it. You know, you'll never have that. I don't think you will" (Episode 12, "What We Know"). Perhaps this is the real power of *Serial*, for the podcast leads us on a journey in which our real focus is no longer upon finding the answer to the mystery but on contemplating the process of cognition and meaning making itself. How do the stories that we tell about ourselves and others speak to our humanity and ethical concerns?

In an interview held at the Peabody Awards, Ira Glass, the editorial advisor for *Serial*, noted that, amidst the conflicting information, the one point that they could assert was that the events central to the prosecution's case could not have happened in the timeline they produced. However, challenging the prosecution's narrative ("taking the narrative back from the prosecution") does not necessarily mean that Syed is innocent. In fact, Adnan has not been able to produce an effective counter-narrative of his own, for his account of his memory of the day that Hae goes missing continues to be vague. Here, we are left with Koenig's paradox. The legal system has not met the burden of proof for Syed's guilt, but that does not mean that Adnan Syed is innocent. In *Serial*'s acoustic space, filled with the irony and ambiguity of the "nuance . . . in people's voices" ("Interview"), the convicting narratives do not necessarily lead to narratives of conviction; rather, we are left with epistemological gaps in a postmodern soundscape—listening, listening for the next possible narrative resolution, the illusory promise of "what we know."

Works Cited

Barthes, Roland. *Image, Music, Text*. Trans. Stephen Heath. New York: Hill and Wang, 1977. Print.

Basu, Tanya, Lenika Cruz, Conor Friedersdorf, and Katie Kilkenny. "*Serial* Episode 10: Did Racism Help Put Adnan in Prison." *The Atlantic*. 4 Dec. 2014. Web. 15 Apr. 2016.

Bergson, Henri. *Matter and Memory*. Trans. N.M. Paul and W.S. Palmer. New York: Zone, 1991. Print.

Connor, Steven. *Dumbstruck: A Cultural History of Ventriloquism*. New York: Oxford University Press, 2001. Print.

Crook, Tim. *Radio Drama: Theory and Practice*. New York: Routledge, 1999. Print.

Derrida, Jacques. *Of Grammatology*. Baltimore: Johns Hopkins University Press, 1976. Print.

Gamerman, Ellen. "*Serial* Podcast Catches Fire." *Wall Street Journal*. 13 Nov. 2014. Web. 1 Apr. 2016.

Kahn, Richard and Douglas Kellner. "Oppositional Politics and the Internet: A Critical/Reconstructive Approach." *Cultural Politics* 1.1 (2005): 75–100. Print.

Kelly, Heather. "*Frozen* and *Serial* Top Apple Best-of-2014 Lists." *CNN*. 8 Dec. 2014. Web. 2 Apr. 2016.

Kermode, Frank. *The Sense of an Ending: Studies in the Theory of Fiction*. Oxford: Oxford University Press, 1967. Print.

Koenig, Sarah. "Update: Adnan Syed's Hearing," February 2016. *Serial, Season One*. Audio podcast. WEBZ, Chicago. 2016. Web. 2 Apr. 2016.

———. Interview with Terry Gross. *Fresh Air*. Natl. Public Radio. WHYY, Philadelphia. 23 Dec. 2014.

———. "2014 Peabody Award Acceptance Speech." *Peabody: Stories that Matter*. May 31, 2015. Web. 2 Apr. 2016.

———. "The Price of Tea, October 5, 2014." *Serial, Season One, Related to Episode Two*. Audio podcast. WEBZ, Chicago. 2014. Web. 2 Apr. 2016.

———. *Serial, Season One*. Audio podcast. WEBZ, Chicago. 2014. Web. 22 Nov. 2015. <http://serialpodcast.org>

Lacey, Kate. *Listening Publics: The Politics and Experience of Listening in the Media Age*. Cambridge: Polity, 2013. Print.

McLuhan, Marshall. *Gutenberg Galaxy: The Making of Typographic Man*. Toronto: U of Toronto P, 1962. Print.

McLuhan, Marshall and Eric McLuhan. *Laws of Media: The New Science*. Toronto: U of Toronto P, 1988. Print.

Miller, Kelsey. "Update: Hae Min Lee's Family Directs New Statement at *Serial* Fans." *Refinery 29*. 8 Feb. 2016. Web. 3 Apr. 2016.

Rajanala, Alekya. "Podcasting—Northwestern and Beyond." *North by Northwestern*. North by Northwestern. 3 Nov. 2015. Web. 30 Dec. 2015.

Seabrook, Andrea. "Adnan Syed Hearing Wrap-Up." Weekend Edition Saturday. Natl. Public Radio. KCRW, Santa Monica. 6 Feb. 2016.

Sweeney, Susan Elizabeth. "The Metaphysical Detective Story." In *Critical Insights: Crime and Detective Fiction*. Ed. Rebecca Martin. Hackensack: Salem, 2013. 176–196. Print.

Verma, Neil. *Theater of the Mind: Imagination, Aesthetics, and American Radio Drama*. Chicago: University of Chicago Press, 2012. Print.

"What '*Serial*'-mania Says about the Growing Popularity of Podcasts." *PBS NEWS-HOUR. NewsHour Productions LLC*. 11 Dec. 2014. Web. 2 Apr. 2016.

Williams, Raymond. *Television : Technology and Cultural Form*. New York: Routledge, 1990. Print.

Wong, Julia Carrie. "The Problem with *Serial* and the Model Minority." *BuzzFeed*. 16 Nov. 2014. Web. 30 Dec. 2015.

6 The Impossible Ethics of *Serial*

Sarah Koenig, Foucault, Lacan

Ryan Engley

Introduction

Many experts and commentators have weighed in on how "ethical" it was for Sarah Koenig to be reporting a story that she had not finished, thus allowing the fissures, inconsistencies, speculations, and tensions of the investigative process into her storytelling as *Serial* episodes began to air. *Serial*'s uniqueness as a cultural object comes from its revival of the serial format for radio storytelling, commonly thought of as more a mid-twentieth-century media phenomenon. The podcast's form has generated both massive interest and critical condemnation. My argument is that the ethics that *Serial* suggests (but doesn't fully embrace) has its basis in an ethics of desire inextricably bound to its structure.

Koenig's reporting—if we are to understand Joyce Barnathan, President of the International Center for Journalists—entails nothing less than an exciting and necessary rupture to the form of traditional journalism. This break from tradition is fundamental to *Serial*'s appeal. Koenig's use of seriality imbues her reporting with the "anxiety" and "soul searching" that, Barnathan notes, is present in the *process* of traditional journalism but absent in the final *product*. Barnathan sees Koenig introducing a new "transparency" to journalism, instilling it with a different kind of credibility.

Yet, what Barnathan sees as "transparency," others see as a breach of fundamental journalistic ethics. For all its formal innovation, the bulk of the ethical criticism levied against *Serial* takes issue with the format. Focusing her concerns on the issue of form, Jessica Goldstein of *Think Progress* interviewed three experts in media ethics: Jane Kirtley, Donna Leff, and Edward Wasserman. Leff thought that the "foremost" obligation of journalists is to "tell the truth," and she conceded that the rest is "art" or "storytelling" (Goldstein). As she says, "[T]hose are questions of taste and art and narrative arc, but I don't think they're about ethics." Leff did worry, however, about potential problems with *Serial*'s end. What if Sarah Koenig *had* discovered Hae Min Lee's *actual* killer? Would she misdirect and tease the narrative to skirt around information she was knowingly withholding from the audience? As Kirtley says, "I don't think there's any problem with continuing your investigation [after finding key information], but I don't like the idea of keeping core information away from the listener" (Goldstein). Would Koenig pretend to have just stumbled upon it? These questions proved to be unfounded, but they are certainly not groundless. For these journalism and ethics scholars, Koenig's approach encouraged distrust, not belief as it did for Barnathan.

Edward Wasserman was perhaps the most skeptical of *Serial*'s radical deployment of seriality (though he did note that it was "riveting"). He writes, "[T]he downside [of releasing information as it is uncovered is if] there are speculations that are being raised that are defamatory, and turn out to be false" (Goldstein). So much of Koenig's reporting is informed by what Barnathan calls "transparency"—the exact thing that makes Wasserman uncomfortable. Goldstein asks Wasserman if there is a way to allay these fears without fundamentally altering *Serial*'s structure. Asked if perhaps the answer is to produce the entire series before airing an episode, Wasserman replies, "This may be the old school me speaking, but I would be more comfortable with that," though he does admit that doing so means "you lose a certain amount of dramatic edge" (Goldstein). Despite the potential for Leff and Kirtley's concern about Koenig manipulating the narrative arc around information she was withholding from the listener being arguably more prevalent in Wasserman's model, his prescription for "solving the ethical problem of *Serial*" is interesting: he wants *Serial* without the serial.[1]

The form of *Serial*—the genre of seriality—ruptures Sarah Koenig's reporting, separating it from traditional journalism or documentary filmmaking. Even regular reporting on the same story (say, a presidential campaign) is not serial; a *sequence* of news items about the same topic, event, or person does not constitute *serial* reporting. The serial reporting practiced by Koenig is a punctuated whole, a chain of installments each deferring a totality of meaning to the next installment. When we talk about seriality, we are concerned with endings (how a story wraps up), and, when we are concerned with endings, we are concerned with narrative and desire. These concerns separate *Serial* from the wider world of journalism of which it is a part, and they require a different understanding of ethical reporting to evaluate.

Serial is not simply a crime drama, told meticulously, or simply entertainment rooted in hard fact. It is not simply a challenge to the justice system, to notions of truth and innocence. It is all of these things, and therefore, I argue, it instantiates its own ethics, an ethics that prior journalistic and documentary models do not help to elucidate. Seriality posits a gap in knowing, a delay in disclosure, an interval in storytelling. Its history is in the literary, but that does not make it opposed to evidence-based investigations of truth. Far from it. *Serial* adroitly employs the gap that seriality introduces in narrative. Koenig uses this gap that the serial form requires to advance an ethics of reporting that is concerned with discovering "the truth" only. Journalists, of course, are concerned with "the truth," but few—if any—other journalists consider truth within a serial narrative structure. This leads Koenig to explore hunches, opine out loud, and reach tentative and journalistically irresponsible conclusions. Contrary to critics, I do not believe this behavior needs to be reined in; it needs to be considered on its own merits and, ultimately, pushed to inhabit its own ethical territory.

To see more fully the ethical territory that *Serial* charts, it is useful to look not at models in the field of journalism but at models in philosophy. First, we will survey the critical conversation surrounding the ethicality of *Serial*'s first season. We will then look to Foucault and his ethics of truth telling known as *parrhesia*. Foucault's notion of *parrhesia* is dependent upon one's relationship with an interlocutor, just as Sarah Koenig's reporting in *Serial*'s first season relies on her relationship with the accused and convicted Adnan Syed (and vice versa). But Foucault alone does not take us far enough. To bring us further—specifically, to the territory of desire—we turn to psychoanalyst Jacques Lacan. What Foucault leaves out of his analysis of *parrhesia* and the ethical position of the interlocutor is exactly the thing that psychoanalysis (and *Serial*) interrogates: the desire of the Other. I argue that it is not possible to consider ethical acts—be they speech acts or otherwise—without a notion of the unconscious desire that subtends supposedly ethical work.

Our reading of Lacan will not strictly be a corrective of Foucault, however. Each thinker's ethical project needs to borrow from crucial elements of the other for the purpose of articulating the ethical ground of *Serial*. We need to make an argument for the unlikely fusion of Foucault and Lacan to see the different conception of ethics that *Serial* instantiates. Then we will move to consider the following: how does that notion of ethics challenge *Serial*, and how does *Serial* challenge that notion of ethics? What can Foucault and Lacan reveal about *Serial*, and what can *Serial* reveal about Foucault and Lacan? By engaging with the ethical project each of these thinkers proffers, we can see that *Serial* uses the "problems" of seriality—the very form of the show itself—to advance a different ethics of journalism, an ethics more concerned with uncovering truth than in being "journalistically responsible."

Serial in Critical Dialogue

Anthropologists Durrani, Gotkin, and Laughlin explore how *Serial*'s expert use of the podcast form might provide a road map for anthropologists to transmit their academic work. The authors see how *Serial* fits—and challenges—anthropology's core tenets as a discipline, particularly as it regards subjectivity and the representation of diverse cultures and communities of color, like, according to the authors, *Serial*'s near "public anthropology" of Muslim Americans problematically told from the singular perspective of a white journalist (595). The authors struggle with balancing the intimacy of Koenig's radio voice and the closeness she feels to the subject of her investigation with her racial and class detachment from it. Commenting on Koenig's analogy of the case to Shakespeare's *Othello* and Adnan as being "not a Moor exactly but a Muslim all the same," they write:

> The fact that Koenig relies on an understanding of Muslimness here that spans from Shakespearean representations of the Moor to Adnan Syed, a Pakistani American from Baltimore, shows that her investments in the politics and ethics of representation do not quite meet the rigorous standards that we, as academics, would like to think that we have for ourselves.
>
> (Durrani et al. 595)

Koenig fails to be detached enough and allows her own cultural history to determine her account.

Others have argued for *Serial* to be granted special dispensation on issues exactly like this. Friedersdorf notes: "White reporters covering minority communities should proceed with great care, thoughtfulness, and sensitivity—and scrutiny of their coverage is important." However, he steadfastly defends the podcast's shortcomings:

> *Serial* is a reflection on a murder case and the criminal-justice system reported over "just" a year, which is to say, it is researched with more effort and depth than 99 percent of journalism produced on any beat in America.

Durrani et al. acknowledge this position—that for whatever criticism Sarah Koenig and *Serial* deserve for the unchecked white privilege operating in the background of the show, we could not even have these rich and important discussions on race, representation, and privilege without *Serial*—but it is clear that they do not support it. What the anthropologists shy away from is part of what made *Serial* such a phenomenon—it took risks. *It is the serial form itself that is at the root of all of these ethical quandaries*. It produces the very narrative element that attracts Durrani et al. to wonder at the potential use of the serial form for their discipline, but it also repels them. The serial form of both releasing information *and speculating about it as it is released* produces the ethical questions that give pause to the authors' analysis and recommendation of the podcast form for anthropology.

What ties all of these concerns together—questions about the form, the dispensing of information, the speculation that is tantamount to public slander, the unacknowledged white privilege—is Sarah Koenig herself. Barnathan defends Koenig's objectivity and transparency: *"As she says, she has no skin in the game.* She is simply looking into a story about a promising high school student of Pakistani origin accused of killing his former girlfriend, Hae Min Lee, an exuberant, talented teenager of Korean descent" (Barnathan, emphasis mine). It is not accurate to say that Koenig has "no skin in the game." In the first episode, "The Alibi," Koenig makes her position in this investigation clear with two statements that virtually bookend the opening entry to *Serial*. Introducing the concept and approach to the series, Koenig says, "I'm not a detective or a private investigator. I'm not even a crime reporter. But, yes, every day this year, I've tried to figure out the alibi of a 17-year-old boy." The episode closes with an email exchange between Koenig and famous missing witness Asia McClain (i.e., "the alibi" in "The Alibi"):

> All this time I thought the courts proved it was Adnan that killed her. I thought he was where he deserved to be. Now I'm not so sure. . . . . I just hope that Adnan isn't some sick bastard just trying to manipulate his way out of jail. *I wrote back, "Believe me, I'm on exactly the same page."*
>
> (Barnathan, emphasis mine)

Koenig positions herself—from the very beginning—as the "lost witness" to the entire case. The first lines of *Serial* are as follows:

> For the last year, I've spent every working day trying to figure out where a high school kid was for an hour after school one day in 1999— or if you want to get technical about it, and apparently I do, where a high school kid was for 21 minutes after school one day in 1999.
>
> (Barnathan)

Her relentless quest to find Adnan's alibi leads to the identification with Asia McClain we see in that snippet from their email exchange—"Believe me, I'm on exactly the same page [with the lost witness]." If *Serial* was *really about* finding "the alibi"—Asia McClain—it could have ended after one episode. It is not, however. It is about Sarah Koenig's attempt to *become* the alibi for Adnan Syed and her struggle with whether that is right, whether Adnan is guilty or innocent. Koenig has a *tremendous* amount of "skin in the game," contrary to Barnathan's assertion, and this is precisely what makes *Serial* so compelling and such a rich site for theory and discourse. We start to see that the ethical question posed by *Serial* is opened up by its form: seriality reveals the process by which a journalist assumes a role in a story. Seriality opens space for relationships to form (journalist to investigation, journalist to subject) and for desire to emerge as a mode of inquiry. *Serial* shows how Foucault's ethics of *parrhesia* and Lacan's ethics of desire emerge through a serial narrative structure. This is the strength of *Serial*, not its ethical blind spot.

Koenig and Foucault

The turn to theory can, at times, seem to be a way to treat abstractly a concrete worldly situation—just as the serializing of a 1999 murder case can seem to turn people into characters and traumatic real-life drama into entertainment— but that is not the case here. I submit that it is only with a proper grasp of what theory can bring to bear on this discussion of ethics that we can truly and fully understand *Serial*. Michel Foucault's work on ethics focuses on the necessity of a relationship with another as the basis for truth telling. Jacques Lacan will trouble Foucault's conception of ethics by introducing the unconscious and desire as fecund territories for ethical inquiry.

Koenig serves as the chief interlocutor for two audiences vital to *Serial*'s narrative development. Both are obvious: Adnan and the listener. Foucault offers a way to help us begin to theorize the contours of ethics, truth telling, and the necessity of the interlocutor. His oeuvre is particularly invested in the criminal or delinquent subject, making him a natural thinker to guide an approach to *Serial*. However, I focus not on concepts such as the Panopticon or a work such as *Discipline and Punish* here but on *parrhesia*—a "modality of truth telling"—most schematically developed in *The Courage of Truth*, a series of lectures conducted at the Collège De France from 1983–1984 (2). Foucault's work on *parrhesia* exerts influence on the fields of politics and law to this day.[2] Philosophical *parrhesia* is "frank speech," the speech exchanged between friends, with an interlocutor whom one risks offending with one's personal truth. Political *parrhesia* is "fearless speech," the truth telling that risks one's position or standing in democracy, as "democracy is not the privileged site of *parrhesia* but the place in which *parrhesia* is the most difficult to practice" (58). This is because *parrhesia* requires truth telling without any hiding and without the rhetorical flourishes that often manifest themselves in the practice of democracy. One's duty, so to speak, is to the truth—not to curate an image, lobby for political advancement, or cover oneself in rhetorical glory. I want to focus on this basic structure for truth telling in *The Courage of Truth*, as it is germane to a discussion of

Serial, a narrative premised on truth telling and truth investigation. It also, usefully, troubles the kind of ethical journalism practiced and implied by Koenig. It allows us to focus on her relationship—interlocutorship, if you will—with Adnan Syed, troubling the ethicality of that utterly fundamental relationship for *Serial*.

As Foucault sees it, truth telling is the basis for the development of an ethics of the self, one in which the self is connected to others: "In ancient culture, and therefore well before Christianity, telling the truth about oneself was an activity involving several people, an activity with other people, and even more precisely an activity with one other person, a practice for two" (5). In line with his characteristic rejection of the institutionalization of religion, Foucault is against the idea that an expert or specialist (like the priest in Catholicism) *needs* to be a part of this truth-telling equation and that confession *needs* to be the model for truth telling itself. Instead, the Other in truth telling requires no special status except being the interlocutor for the self.

Koenig proves time and time again to be the *perfect* interlocutor for Adnan. They speak freely and easily. It is engaging to listen to. As a listener, I feel as if these two have a real relationship, beyond "interviewer and interviewee," a relationship that is well positioned—in our Foucauldian formulation—to explore truth. Truth, for Foucault, is in no way equivalent to *objective fact*, a similarity his ethical philosophy shares with the nature of *Serial*'s investigation. The recitation of formulae or rules, for example, does not count as "truth." *Parrhesia*—truth telling—is a position one adopts in regard to the truth, to speaking it, to investigating it. *Parrhesia* demands that the individual risk the self in the act of telling the truth. This risk of offending or challenging the Other stands as the measuring stick for the effectiveness of the act of *parrhesia*. Speaking truth by necessity incurs backlash, censure, rejection. The investigation of truth, as we see in *Serial*, must be vulnerable to the very attacks levied against it that we saw above. Equally true, Koenig and Syed's relationship must be vulnerable and open to risk.

There is, however, a significant exchange between Koenig and Syed that adheres almost exactly to Foucault's "*parrhesiastic* game." Koenig reports that after six months of speaking to Adnan over the phone, he asked her what her interest was in the case. She rifles through a list of things she thought were interesting about the case and finally says, "[W]hat really hooked me most, was him. Just trying to figure out, who is this person who says he didn't kill this girl but is serving a life sentence for killing this girl" ("The Case against Adnan Syed"). Koenig's answer results in, as she says, the closest thing to a "hostile" interaction they had while working on *Serial*—it is also the moment where we see that Syed is the perfect interlocutor for Koenig herself.

She tells Adnan that she thinks he's "a really nice guy" and that she likes talking to him, that driving her interest in the case is figuring out "what does that mean?" Sarah is attempting to reconcile how much she enjoys Adnan's conversation and company with the idea that he is also a violent killer. Adnan pauses a while before responding: a silence that is remarkable for their communication simply for its exceptional status. Adnan is flustered and stutters his way toward eventually saying, "[I]t's weird to hear you say that because, I don't even really know you" (Koenig). Taken aback, Sarah asks, "[A]re you saying I don't know you at all?" (Koenig). Adnan is still incredulous that Sarah can make the judgment that he is "a nice person," given that they have talked on the phone only "a few times" (more than thirty hours by this point, which Koenig points out is "way more than I've talked to a lot of people I think I know. People I consider friends" [Koenig]).

There is a lot in this interaction: further affirmation that, yes, Koenig does have *quite a lot* of "skin in the game," as she more or less tells Adnan (and the listener) that she considers him a friend; Adnan is engaging in *parrhesia* (frank speech), risking his good standing with Koenig, his interlocutor, who could be his savior or executioner (as Adnan refers to Koenig in another episode). The stated point of *Serial*'s investigation is to find "missing evidence" or question the evidence that exists. If the convicted murderer outright tells the person taking new interest in his decades-old conviction that "you don't know really know me," that's as convincing an argument for "maybe he *did* do it" as Adnan could have offered. Simply put, it makes it easier to believe this "nice guy" could have killed somebody if he brazenly tells the person investigating his conviction, "I know you think you know me, but you do not."

We do, however, encounter a problem with Foucault here. The skeptical reader will ask, but does Adnan know he's speaking *parrhesiastically*? Wouldn't one have to have knowledge of one's ethical act before doing it? Or is it that the ethical act is a matter of retroactive interpretation? Foucault's entire system of truth telling and ethical speech/action is premised on an unstated and untenable notion of intention. In Foucault, we can read intention directly from actions. That is, if one practices *parrhesia* as Foucault describes, one is ethical. We do not question the motivations and machinations of the interlocutor if the interlocutor's actions fit the system that Foucault details. Foucault famously rejects the insights of psychoanalysis—particularly its call for, as he might term it, a "hermeneutics of the subject." If the entire psychoanalytic project had to be boiled down to a singular idea, it would be this: people do not do things for the reasons they think they do them. One need not be an ardent reader of Freud or Lacan to accept this idea; one need believe not even in an *un*conscious but, merely, in a *sub*conscious.

Foucault utterly rejects this. There is no unconscious lurking in the background of Foucault's work and thought. It matters not the reason behind Koenig openly questioning Syed's character while on the phone with him; the only thing that matters is *that she did it.* By affixing the locus of logic on one's relation to others, in the way Foucault explores, the intention doesn't matter—rather, the willingness to begin acting *parrhesiastically* as part of a *process*. The "intention" arises as a result of practice, or *askesis*, in Foucault's terminology. This seems like a perfectly Foucauldian answer to the problem that he, sadly, did not live long enough to confront. It is, however, an answer that is open to psychoanalytic appraisal, which is to say that if intent can be apprehended only through a process that reveals in the rearview, then *parrhesiastic* acts and utterances acquire meaning through the very same process that speech does during a psychoanalytic session—retroactively. And if meaning only emerges retroactively, this implies that the gap within utterances—precisely what the serial form privileges—marks an interruption in our truth-telling practice. In this moment of interruption, the subject's unconscious intention or desire manifests itself. The interruption trumps the truth of our practice with the truth of the subject's desire. In this way, the serial (and *Serial*) takes us beyond Foucault, who admits no theory of desire, and to the terrain of psychoanalysis.

Koenig *avec* Lacan

While Foucault appears to be a natural resource for a discussion of the ethical speech that can arise between interlocutors, his ideas stumble when we consider the desire that might be at work in that relationship—a critical factor in *Serial* and the ethical project I'm locating in its first season. While the issue of intention is an impediment in Foucault, it is a site for theorization in French psychoanalyst Jacques Lacan. In *The Courage of Truth*, Foucault thinks alongside Ancient Greek philosophy, culture, and the "practices" at work in everyday life in an attempt to develop his notion of *parrhesia*. Lacan, starting with his seventh seminar, *The Ethics of Psychoanalysis*, takes aim at what he calls "traditional ethics" emanating from the ancient world, specifically in the work of Aristotle. Traditional ethics aims at "the service of goods" or attends to the good at the expense of desire, according to Lacan (314). Lacan's work, then, stands in opposition to Foucault's project, which has a theory of the ethical act but no theory of intention, a theory of pleasure with no theory of desire.

Lacan famously asks and examines, *Che voui?* or "What do you want?" This is the question posed to the Other that inaugurates the subject's desire.[3] In *Serial*, this question is implicit and undergirds much of Koenig and her team's investigation in the first season. Why didn't Cristina Gutierrez contact Asia McClain? Why didn't Adnan mention speaking to Asia at the library? Why does Jay change his account of the crime over and over again? What do these people *want*? (What does the Other want?) The audience asks this question of Koenig, and she asks this question of everyone and everything she encounters. The issue of desire is here woven into the very fabric of *Serial*'s narrative.

How does desire offer Lacan a "way out" of traditional ethics, and how does the immanent presence of desire separate *Serial* from traditional journalism? Lacan begins, in *The Ethics of Psychoanalysis*, by claiming that "a radical repudiation of a certain ideal of the good is necessary" (230). This ideal of "the good" comes straight from Aristotle and traditional ethics, an ethics preoccupied with, according to Lacan, "[t]he cleaning up of desire, modesty, temperateness, that is to say, the middle path we see articulated so remarkably in Aristotle" (314). Lacan wishes to break with this notion of the ethical being tied to the advancement of the good.

For Lacan, Kant marks the breaking point from the ancient morality of the good. Kant enables us to consider ethical acts regardless of the contribution that they might make to what people today refer to as "flourishing." As he turns ethics away from the good, Kant also turns it away from the merely possible toward the dimension of desire that centers on "the real *qua* impossible," as Zupančič notes. Through his reading of Kant, Lacan allows us to see that the criticism that Koenig breached objective journalistic standards is not viable, or, if it is, it relies on separating desire from the ethical (as in traditional and Foucauldian ethics). Since desire is at the core of the subject, "not giving ground relative to one's desire"—Lacan's ethical maxim—is perfectly sensible. This does not fit *exactly* with the ethical territory I have been crafting for *Serial* and Sarah Koenig. I am adamant that her desire needs to be present in her investigation. Rather than "compromising" her ethical position, this enables and constitutes it.

The Adnan Syed–Sarah Koenig relationship enables truth telling, as we learn from Foucault. It does not enable "verification bias," as some detractors have argued, nor does it compromise Sarah Koenig's objectivity (Friedersdorf, Lafrance, Basu, and Kilkenny). A belief in some objectivity, here, is the lie. Hearns-Branaman calls for new theories on journalism's epistemology. The heart of his project is finding a way to theorize objectivity rather than simply name it. He rejects any approach that resembles a taxonomy. Significantly, his route to new thinking on objectivity and truth in journalism passes through Lacan. It is not hard to understand why. Yes, there must be *some* notion of objectivity that supports journalistic inquiry, but to argue that there is "objective journalism" on the one hand and then that there is *Serial* is to pretend that desire does not complicate *any* other reporting. *Serial* simply *invites* this complication to drive its investigative narrative.

We come finally to a consideration of seriality as such, the form that generates Koenig's ethics. In *Encore*, Lacan's revision of his first ethics seminar, he has made a subtle shift. As Copjec glosses, "[Lacan's] ethics takes off from the proposal that being is not-all or there is no whole of being" (6). In a sense, this is what *Serial* offers us. What inheres in seriality is the gap. This gap in knowing, the gap in meaning, of possibility. This gap raises expectations and, of course, disappointment. This is what endows the serial with its particular character, and this is what *Serial*'s detractors do not reckon with: the way its form informs the investigation is the podcast's highest virtue. As Foucault says, "*parrhesia* . . . is only [*parrhesia*] after it has opened up an essential, fundamental, and structurally necessary moment of the possibility of hatred and rupture" (25). Foucault and Lacan both acknowledge the structural necessity for a gap to be present for the ethical to emerge.[4] This gap is utterly constitutive of the serial, and it is what has made *Serial* so fascinating for those who extol it (like Barnathan) and those who take issue with it (like Wasserman).

Conclusion

Serial intervenes at the unexpected intersections of narrative and the law, journalism and desire, ethics and seriality. It has been hailed for pioneering a new journalistic format (the podcast) and for saving an old one (radio). It has been criticized for its unchecked and unacknowledged white privilege, its sensationalizing of a murder, its flouting of established journalistic convention, and its potential bias toward the convicted felon at the heart of it all. The question of *Serial*'s ethics pervades all of these questions.

What cannot be debated regarding Koenig and *Serial*, however, is that what the show does is *new*. As such, I have argued that *Serial* requires a different framework to evaluate its ethical content since it is outside the bounds of established critique. In a standard documentary series (such as Netflix's *Making a Murderer*) or published works of journalism, the journalist is not the active interlocutor of the subject of the story (here, Adnan Syed). For this reason, we need a model for evaluating the ethical status of the relationship between Koenig and Syed that drives *Serial*'s investigation. For insight into this new framework, I have turned to Foucault and Lacan, whose ostensibly incompatible thought is indispensable. Despite the problem of intention at the heart of Foucault's ethics of *parrhesia* that *Serial* allows us to see, his model is exemplary for showing how the interlocutor makes ethical speech possible.

Critics have opined that Koenig becomes too close to Syed, clouding her ability to evaluate his case objectively. Foucault would say that such objectivity risks nothing. Were Koenig to be removed from Syed partially or completely, there would be much less to pull her toward the opinion that Syed is innocent. A dispassionate investigation into the physical material of a possible wrongful conviction is certainly a valuable practice, but it can by no means be considered the only way to investigate truth. There must be alternatives available. *Serial is this alternative.* The question that none of Koenig's detractors have asked is this: what does it mean if "responsible journalism" is opposed to the investigation of truth? Koenig and former consulting homicide detective Jim Trainum say that the detectives on Syed's case "probably settled for what was good enough to be the truth" ("To Be Suspected"). But *Serial* does not settle for this. If "responsible journalism" would separate Koenig from Syed, prevent her from interviewing certain people, prevent her from airing her speculations and accusations as they occur in her investigation—distance her from the truth, in other words—then what is the ethical status of this supposed "responsible journalism"? The issue of *Serial*'s ethics cannot be so black and white as to rely on conventional models that fail to meet *Serial* on its own ground (i.e., confront what it is actually doing).

These questions are fortified by Lacan, with whom we are able to look at the ethical status of desire. It is clear that Koenig desires—if not to clear Adnan Syed of wrongdoing entirely—to be the person who can know definitively what happened in this murder case. Without a doubt, Koenig realized that her desire to find the exculpatory evidence that would prove Adnan's innocence compromised her journalistic voice—a desire that, as I have argued, leads her to position herself as this "lost" expert witness. But even as this compromises traditional notions of "journalistic integrity," it increases narrative tension and listener interest in the show. Crucially, it pushes Koenig toward a different territory of ethics, one that sheds traditional notions of objectivity.

Perhaps the most enticing and disquieting element for some listeners has been the narrative aspect of the series. Even Koenig tries to separate herself from the intersection of narrative and law that subtends *Serial*: "I'll present what my reporting bears out, and that's my responsibility . . . not to entertain you with some wonderful, perfect ending. I don't mean that in a holier-than-thou way at all—it's just—I'm a reporter" (cited in Gamerman). Here, Koenig struggles with the ethics of seriality and desire that her podcast develops—we even see seriality displacing Koenig's reporting from herself. Koenig's statement fails to grapple with the space her podcast created for her: this impossible hybridity of reporter and storyteller, interlocutor and subject of desire, distanced from traditional journalism. In other words, if the principal author does not fully embrace the narrative aspect of *Serial*, how can Wasserman? By insisting "I'm just a reporter," Koenig refuses the radicality of her own project. That Koenig is even being *asked* about her "series finale" alerts us to the uniqueness of her journalism. Further, by recoiling from the full narrative import of *Serial*, Koenig misses a crucial insight graspable in her listeners' worry: the potential for disappointment is increased with serial endings over episodic endings. I contend that disappointment is the *virtue* of serial storytelling. Serial storytelling is so enriching, so engrossing, because it raises ever higher our expectations for it. Fans worried about the ending being a letdown *is the point*. One can only be disappointed because of the form. It raises expectations and then (usually) disappoints, but this is a far more valuable narrative dynamic than one that meets requirements without ever raising them. This, perhaps more than any other element of the podcast, is what definitively separates *Serial* from traditional and everyday news reporting.

Indeed, what keeps Koenig's "I think the case is weak but I don't know if Adnan is guilty or not" final statement from being disappointing is that the case (as of this writing) is *still active*. Adnan will now face another day in court. There may be more *Serial* (Season One). The possibility of more, the deferment of the ending, the possibility of more possibilities, is the only thing that keeps the serial from disappointing. As psychoanalysis has it, complete satisfaction is an impossibility; were one to be completely satisfied, one would stop desiring. And who would want to stop desiring a narrative whose form asks us, problematically, to continually reencounter it?

Notes

1. While, yes, a prerecorded investigation of twelve episodes aired week by week is still *serialized*, such a thing would lack the *live serial* aspect of what Koenig and her crew offered millions of listeners. The "live" aspect of *Serial* opened a gap in the narrative that most serialized-after-production stories close down. Removing it would not simply cause *Serial* to "lose dramatic edge"; it would cleave from *Serial* the very thing that made every listener feel like they were thinking, feeling, speculating, conjecturing, wondering right along with Koenig. In short, the series would lack the very reason Wasserman was contacted to comment on it in the first place.
2. See Simon.
3. Lacanian psychoanalysis is premised on the idea that our desire is not our own—our desire is always aimed at the Other. Lacan begins this thread of thought simply: when you're a kid and you make your parents laugh, you don't know why they're laughing, but it makes them happy, so you keep doing whatever it is that makes them happy, even though you do not really understand it. Children are thrown into a world full of the "secret" codes of symbolic interaction (e.g., *not* actually answering "How are you?" when one says that to you on the street), so one's whole way of relating to the world occurs in this very matrix—yes, I know exactly what to do to appear normal in public, but I don't know why I need to or want to. What we are looking for, according to psychoanalysis, is the Other's approval.
4. If the psychoanalytic subject is the subject of desire, the Foucauldian subject (he would prefer "individual") comes into being through "the historical analysis

of the limits imposed upon us and an experiment with the possibility of going beyond them" ("What Is Enlightenment," *Ethics, Subjectivity and Truth* 319). The subject who exceeds her or his historical limits is the ethical subject, the *parrhesiast*, but it is not the case that this is an *excessive subject* as it would be in Lacan and in psychoanalysis. The desire that exceeds biological or even situational necessity is not present in Foucault. We still have this flattening of speech and act—result—with intention. For us, Lacan offers a way out of this problem in Foucault. Indeed, with Lacan—in working with excess, enjoyment, and desire—we see a better fit for discussing the ethics of the serial form that arises through Koenig's reporting in *Serial*.

Works Cited

Barnathan, Joyce. "Why *Serial* Is Important for Journalism." *Columbia Journalism Review*. Columbia Journalism Review, 25 Nov. 2014. Web. 13 May 2016.

Copjec, Joan. *Imagine There's No Woman: Ethics and Sublimation*. Cambridge, MA: MIT, 2004. Print.

Durrani, Mariam, Kevin Gotkin and Corrina Laughlin. "*Serial*, Seriality, and the Possibilities for the Podcast Format." *American Anthropologist* 117.3 (2015): 587–598. Web.

Foucault, Michel. *The Courage of Truth: The Government of Self and Others II: Lectures at the Collège De France 1983–1984*. Ed. Frédéric Gros. Trans. Graham Burchell. Basingstoke, Hampshire: Palgrave Macmillan, 2011. Print.

Friedersdorf, Conor. "The Backlash against *Serial*—and Why It's Wrong." *The Atlantic*. Atlantic Media Company, 3 Dec. 2014. Web. 15 May 2016.

Friedersdorf, Conor, Adrienne Lafrance, Tanya Basu and Katie Kilkenny. "*Serial* Episode 8: A Study in Bias?" *The Atlantic*. Atlantic Media Company, 13 Nov. 2014. Web. 15 May 2016.

Gamerman, Ellen. "*Serial* Podcast Catches Fire." *The Wall Street Journal*. Dow Jones & Company, 13 Nov. 2014. Web. 15 May 2016.

Goldstein, Jessica. "The Complicated Ethics of *Serial*, the Most Popular Podcast of All Time." *Think Progress*. Center for American Progress Action Fund, 20 Nov. 2014. Web. 14 May 2016.

Hearns-Branaman, Jesse Owen. *Journalism and the Philosophy of Truth: Beyond Objectivity and Balance*. New York: Routledge, 2016. Print. Routledge Research in Journalism.

Koenig, Sarah. "*Serial*: Season One." *Serial*. WEBZ Chicago. 2014.

Lacan, Jacques. *The Seminar of Jacques Lacan. The Ethics of Psychoanalysis*. Trans. Dennis Porter. New York: Norton, 1992. Print.

Simon, Jonathan. "Fearless Speech in the Killing State: The Power of Capital Crime Victim Speech." *North Carolina Law Review* 82 (2003): 1377–1414. Print.

Zupančič, Alenka. *Ethics of the Real: Kant, Lacan*. London: Verso, 2004. Print.

7 *Serial*'s Aspirational Aesthetics and Racial Erasure

Charli Valdez

The podcast *Serial* triggered, unsurprisingly, familiar concerns about the ethics of aestheticizing something akin to "true crime," but did the podcast really take advantage of the tragedy suffered by Lee's family and the larger community? The program's runaway success exacerbated this concern. An @iTunesPodcasts tweet of November 14, 2014, announced that *Serial* had reached five million downloads faster than any other podcast. By April of 2016, it had surpassed 200 million downloads (Gambini). Koenig herself admits to being surprised at how much of a breakout success it became—in other words, surprised at just how resonant the aesthetic techniques were. This particular concern about aestheticizing true crime has also garnered some traction, given the high ethical waterline, or at least the "high" cultural ranking, of NPR as compared to the made-for-television, guilty-pleasure crime shows and police dramas. The responsible and non-sensational reporting that NPR is known for shapes the project profoundly. Indeed, *Serial* is an aspirational examination of, and intervention in, a possible miscarriage of justice. A second, and overlapping, polemic about *Serial* involves the question of privilege and racial erasure in the podcast. For example, in attending to Adnan Syed's Muslim identity, Koenig is careful to consider the religious and cultural implications of that identity, but she goes absolutely silent on the interconnected racial dimension. What if we were to couch these two polemics in the context of critical race theory?

Critical race theory has its roots in critical legal studies, a legal approach that sprang from a 1977 conference at the University of Wisconsin–Madison and that holds first and foremost that the law is political and never neutral. Critical race theory, in turn, departs from theories regarding the social construction of race and the rhetorical efficacy of storytelling. Derrick Bell contends that the liberal "success" of the civil rights movement and other liberal institutions should be problematized. He pioneered the methodologies associated with critical race theory, using fictional stories to great rhetorical effect. Critical race theory isn't simply storytelling, however, and I will briefly review three of the more common tenets of critical race theory below: counterstory, the disclosure of ignored realities, and narrative analysis.

Richard Delgado writes that "critical race theorists have built on everyday experience with perspective, viewpoint, and the power of stories and persuasion to come to a deeper understanding of how Americans see race. They have written parables, autobiography, and 'counterstories'" that serve to counter widely received narratives in value-laden contexts (44). The forms that these counterstories take are also variable, sometimes composite fictions drawn from several individuals' actual histories, sometimes personal.

Counterstories can be effective especially in situations where the parties involved need to be made literate in the matter at hand. Such stories seek to reveal "ignored or alternative realities" (Delgado 45), redress "embedded preconceptions that marginalize others or conceal their humanity" (48), and speak truth to the one-sided histories that undergird the unexamined ideologies and the decision making of juries, judges, and lawyers. Beyond correcting such profound ignorance, the storytelling rhetoric that critical race theory expounds seeks to lend a voice to the subaltern and provide some relief, or community, in acknowledging that individuals aren't alone when experiencing patterns of systemic discrimination. Telling stories never heard before and sharing perspectives not part of the widely received narrative about this country effect a cultural change on the issue of race and work toward building racial literacy. Delgado writes, "Stories can give [minority communities] voice and reveal that others have similar experiences. Stories can name a type of discrimination; once named it can be combated" (49). This approach is at once pragmatic and laddered, recognizing a fundamental ignorance that cannot be addressed simply by following existing laws that are predicated on that very same ignorance, lack of experience, and limited racial perspective.

Finally, Delgado notes how narrative theory, narrative analysis specifically, informs practitioners of law: "[S]storytelling and narrative analysis [help] to understand how the dynamics of persuasion operate in the courtroom . . . [and] the interplay of power and interpretive authority between lawyer and client" (51). Narrative analysis enables a lawyer to understand and parse better how the story of her or his client unfolds in the courtroom and the effect it has on judge and jury. Such analysis can also reveal power dynamics between people in the courtroom that weren't previously being acknowledged.

To consider how these tenets of critical race theory might shape how we respond to the charges that *Serial* irresponsibly and unethically aestheticizes true crime, I will focus on two important criticisms that have been made. First, however, we must ask: what is meant when we speak of aestheticizing true crime?

A quick discussion of the aesthetic qualities of *Serial* might include characterization, Koenig's stylized NPR voice, and an approach that invites the audience to participate in the reasoning, judgment, and even investigation. Sarah Koenig and *Serial*'s team are well versed in narrative techniques, perspective, voice, and rhetorical analysis. These are the tools that they bring to bear when they investigate the investigation of Adnan.

The issue of aestheticizing true crime isn't limited to *Serial*. In fact, if anything, it finds its way to *Serial* from a larger criticism of the genre itself. Widely recognized as a critical and core dilemma, the aesthetic level of crime drama helps to create guilty pleasure. What about the true-crime genre allows for viewers to dismiss the anxiety that they're taking pleasure in someone's pain? Browder suggests that true-crime books are a popular arena for metaphysical discussions about the nature of evil, the meaning of retribution, and the impossibility of knowing another person. Koenig engages in all these questions. In a sense, then, *Serial* is very much within the genre. Browder notes that "perceived factuality removes the responsibility for aestheticizing violence from both the writer and the reader of such works" (125). In the podcast, there's a pronounced emphasis not merely on the factuality of everything from cell towers to timelines but on a dissection of those facts and an insistence on not blinking in the face of difficult and damning evidence. Koenig's thorough investigation of the facts can be understood as exculpatory of the producers' and readers' guilt, but there might be more at play as well.

The first criticism of *Serial* I'll address speaks to the question of characterization specifically. Wallace-Wells contends that privilege is a problem in the podcast:

> Not racial privilege, exactly, but the more basic privilege that a nonfiction storyteller enjoys, to aestheticize real life, to wonder why all the details don't fit, to say what makes sense and what doesn't—the privilege, most of all, to explain to the world what these people were like . . .

Wallace-Wells qualifies this as relatively unexamined "psychological tourism," the privilege to pass judgment on the very real people caught up in the unfortunate plot. Because this is an accusation that you can assert against all journalism and nonfiction, this criticism loses its edge. There is no uncertain privilege in Koenig rendering the characters here, but Wallace-Wells tellingly dismisses the main point at the outset. This is "exactly" racial privilege at play here: an all-white team, produced in a predominately white medium and subgenre, characterizing persons of color.

Dockterman questions the "cliffhangers" and the lack of resolution as she mounts the second criticism of *Serial* on which I want to focus. She criticizes the public (and popular) disclosure regarding the struggle with personal bias. She cites Kirtley's concern that, unlike traditional investigative journalism, narrative journalism raises an inherent question about how candid one is being with the audience. Dockterman suggests that Koenig "buried the lead."

The criticism of the lack of resolution in Season One of *Serial* seems short sighted. If the audience finds that the podcast ends without resolution, they've missed the whole point in search of the guilty pleasure that a cop show might offer—namely, the notion that there is one-hundred-percent certainty everywhere and one-hundred-percent objectivity when bias isn't being disclosed. *Serial*, on the other hand, culminates clearly and, in the cleverest turn of phrase, with reasonable doubt. Koenig places heavy emphasis on the meta-discussion, tracking her own thinking, doubts, suspicions, and reactions. Levin notes that Haglund calls this "show-your-work" journalism, and Levin praises its "radical transparency." This is the point, in fact. That transparency, on an aesthetic level, invites the listener into the narrative, a successful technique in this case, as testified to by the Reddit responses and record downloads if nothing else. That transparency also reminds listeners that journalists can't avoid bias.

Finally, Dockterman cites Kirtley to criticize *Serial*'s game of "hide the ball." Kirtley's concern centers on how this differs from "traditional investigative journalism" and how it "raises a fundamental question about how candid are you being with your audience about what you knew and when you knew it" (Dockterman). Critical race theory can help parse this question as well because the project of *Serial* isn't simply investigative journalism but one of clearly disclosed counterstory, investigation of ignored reality, and narrative analysis. To achieve this, it engages in a number of narrative techniques, borrowing from a number of genres, or disciplines, beyond traditional investigative journalism. To begin with, from its very title, it cites and partakes in the conventions of true crime. Koenig speaks at one point of not being a true detective as her team acts like a detective in investigating the investigation and trial of Adnan. Finally, *Serial* passes a judgment in the final episode, like a jury would, and, from the beginning, Koenig is quite clear about how suspicious she is of the conviction of Adnan, positioning herself like a lawyer who shapes facts for rhetorical and narrative effect. Kirtley's concern is with how problematic the podcast is as investigative journalism, but *Serial* is fusing true crime, detective work, jury decision making, and lawyerly rhetoric. Nevertheless, even if this were not a concern for Kirtley, it is possible Koenig withheld that judgment of reasonable doubt, intentional fallacies aside, but the effect of her constantly questioning narrative is to wend and wind through evidence and considerations, to seek certainty only to be stumped as the show progressed, and not flinch in the face of that. Koenig was never hiding her doubt; to the contrary, the point was to be perfectly candid about it. It framed the entire podcast. In fact, Dockterman undermines her own point when she later notes the lack of resolution of, and complaints regarding, the ending of *Serial*. The same can't be said of *The Jinx*.

Dockterman's failure to parse the difference between *The Jinx*'s and *Serial*'s endings is predicated in part on a simple premise of purity, suggesting that, normally, investigative journalists don't have to make decisions about what to disclose and about how to order their story and give rhetorical shape to the layout of their investigation. Levin writes, "A typical in-depth reporting project is a poker game where the writer keeps his cards hidden." Koenig's "radical transparency" breaks from that dynamic, and Levin praises her due diligence and the "thoroughness [that] is a journalist's core obligation." Koenig's radical transparency rebuts the notion that there is actual objectivity not only in journalism but in law itself. A central concern of Derrick Bell is how "[d]ecisions about the relevance of distinguishing facts are value-laden and dependent upon a judge's own experiences" (Bell, Delgado, and Stefancic 74). This is simply a reality for journalists and judges alike. Koenig's candid radical transparency merely underscores that fact.

What does this radical transparency look like, and what does it enable the audience to do? At the end of the first episode, Koenig includes a shockingly confessional segment that probably would have been deleted by another editor on another kind of program. In it, she naively expresses surprise at Adnan's nonplussed, tired reaction to the revelation that Koenig had found and talked with Asia. It's easy enough to both cringe and marvel at this segment. Koenig, in a revelatory act of full disclosure, cuts this into the episode. While the editorial decision to include this part can open the door to criticism of that revealed naiveté, it is refreshingly, radically candid and, given that it is a deliberately selected inclusion, opens space for criticism of the kind of privilege for which Koenig stands accused. Including that segment is honest, self-deprecatory, and strategic. And if a critic focuses merely on the individual author (Koenig) of the space that was created in order to engage in that criticism in the first place, that critic might have missed the larger self-sacrificing point.

As Melissa Maerz notes, because of Koenig's self-disclosing ethic, the audience is able to meditate on the issue of complicity. It is an invitation, rendered in first-person point-of-view, and a challenge. Koenig's strategic generosity regarding counter-arguments serves the underlying project of asking if there was a miscarriage of justice and if Adnan is really innocent. It can also be understood as influencing the "perceived factuality" (Browder 125) of *Serial*. Adnan objects to this at 12:50 in Episode 11. His concern is that she is depicting him unfairly by questioning every position that he takes, while she accepts the positions of others she interviews. He accuses her of having a double standard, and he has a point. It does at times feel as if she's willing to believe what others say, while she doubts and investigates all the possible deceptions he may be perpetuating. There is a persuasive rhetorical effect to this approach, however, that opens room for Koenig's main findings to work.

All this is well and fine, but does anything change once we situate *Serial* behind the lens of critical race theory? As delineated earlier, storytelling is at the heart of this methodology, and Koenig and her team are professional storytellers. There are a number of rhetorical gains to be made in storytelling, but this mode can be especially important in skeptical, cynical, and suspicious environments. Storytelling can engage an individual's capacity to suspend disbelief, a notion that Bell advances. If the storyteller has a legal or rhetorical end in mind, the fabric of plot, characterization, and all the aesthetic aspects to the story can occupy the listener's attention while a point is being made. The latter point is important because this isn't simply storytelling; it is storytelling with an agenda. It is counter-storytelling.

Jake Flanagin counterposes "low brow" shows such as Investigation Discovery network's programming (which is "low-rent" and "kitschy and riveting—the ultimate guilty pleasure") to *Serial* (which buys into a public interest in the social importance of a story like Adnan's): "*Serial* dug deep into people's preconceived notions surrounding interracial dating, Muslim-American culture, modern teen masculinity, and the pressure on law enforcement to build clean narratives around crimes." There is a qualitative difference between *Serial*'s investigation into, meditation upon, and exposure of these issues and the "low-brow" version that elides these issues, focusing instead on the sensational, the spectacle, and the pornographic, in Audre Lorde's articulation of the term.

As I noted previously, one fundamental tenet of critical race theory is the disclosure of ignored realities, and, while the podcast *Serial* is not—strictly speaking—courtroom rhetoric, in Episodes 1 and 2, as it parses the court's case regarding Adnan's motive, it does touch upon the ignored realities of Adnan's Muslim community. Durrani et al. write, "Given both the popularity of the podcast and the dearth of media representations of Muslim Americans, *Serial* has become a form of public anthropology about these minority communities" (595). Koenig and her team, professional storytellers to be sure, humanize Syed and seek to name and illuminate a specific legal failing in contemporary U.S. society by drawing attention to the systemic overdetermination of Muslim identity. In other words, in a world in which the audience is submitted to gross mischaracterizations of the Muslim community again and again, *Serial*'s take on the community is a welcome break from that. While this representation of the Muslim community is "refreshing" in many ways (Durrani 595), the bar isn't set very high in such a context, and, as will be seen, Durrani's praise doesn't reflect the full and complex response to *Serial*'s treatment of Muslims, "immigrants," and race.

Another tenet of critical race theory urges that one must also name the discrimination before it can be addressed. The invocation may be truist and a little baggy, but, applied to the case of Adnan's conviction, Koenig commits to naming and combating the discrimination carefully and methodically across twelve episodes. Once named, discrimination can be combated. Koenig's naming of the ineffective defense in Syed's case has led to a judge vacating the sentence in June of 2016, an assessment that as of August 2016 was being appealed by the Maryland Attorney General. The counterstory that Koenig and others developed to expose what went untold in Syed's legal case became part of the unofficial and official legal narrative as attested to by its breakout, genre-changing success and (in part through the knock-on crowdsourced amateur investigation and rhetorical brainstorming) impact on the legal outcome of the case. Despite having originated as a text outside of the legal system and those decisions that it speaks to, it has since story-told its way into the legal system.

Storytelling, of course, is at its heart an aesthetic act. *Serial*—as an aspirational podcast, inviting the Innocence Project into the narrative—aestheticizes not simply to commodify and profit from a tragedy but to effect change as well. The characterization that Wallace-Wells objects to and the supposed cliffhangers that Dockterman dislikes would be two such aesthetic strategies. Who is Koenig to speak for Adnan? If being a responsible journalist doesn't get her a pass on this question, then it must be said that, in revealing the ignored reality of Muslim communities around the country, she must develop Adnan into a fully realized character in order for the integrity of the investigative project to succeed.

Serial fares well in the above due-diligence review. Looking through the lens of critical race theory, turning from the narrative, aesthetic, and critical aspects of the podcast's methodology, how does its racial methodology hold up? Critical race theory does not shy from criticizing anything, including the gains, lauded by the left, of the Civil Rights Acts of the 1960s, which "only address instances of overt discrimination" (Bell et al. 120). Nobody appears to suggest that *Serial* is overtly racist. In point of fact, the charges of racism and privilege against *Serial* engage in tight textual analysis to unpack the subtlety of the discrimination that emerges.

There is a range of reactions to the role of race in *Serial*. Jay Caspian Kang investigates Koenig's investigation of the Syed investigation. Kang adroitly points out how Koenig, in the second episode, creates a rhetorical racial assumption. Adnan states: "You know, it was really easy to date someone that kind of lived within the same parameters that I did." Note that

Adnan does not qualify what he means by those parameters. Kang points out how Koenig assumes that Adnan means the parameters of being an "immigrant." Koenig continues, painting Hae Min Lee's Korean parents as controlling because of their cultural background without any evidence to make such a point.

There is little visual reference in *Serial*'s online appendices to how race is embodied in the individuals who populate the story. Nor does Koenig speak directly to this issue. Chaudry, in Kang's article, says:

> You have an urban jury in Baltimore city, mostly African American, maybe people who identify with Jay [an African-American friend of Syed's who is the state's seemingly unreliable star witness] more than Adnan, who is represented by a community in headscarves and men in beards. . . . The visuals of the courtroom itself leaves an impression and there's no escaping the racial implications there.

On Koenig's part, there is close analysis, for example, of the visual relevance of where the body is found, but the visual manifestation of race is elided. Isn't this, in and of itself, a white privilege? Kang's citation of Chaudry continues: "I don't know to what extent someone who hasn't grown up in a culture can really understand that culture. . . . I think Sarah tried to get it, but I don't know if she ever really did." Kang suggests that Koenig is ultimately unable to transcend the role of cultural tourist. In such exclusions and given the lack of even the discussion of why it might be relevant to exclude such material, Koenig's white privilege is disappointingly apparent.

It may be more than that, however, as there are signs that *Serial*'s racial shortsightedness is aesthetically strategic. Ironically, the professional storytelling and aestheticization of the narrative, mobilized very much in a spirit parallel to that of critical race theory, may be precisely what's behind some of the worst violations regarding the season's treatment of race and racial identities. There is vacillation and suspect ambivalence. While Episode 2 emphasizes Adnan's Muslim identity and Lee's Korean family, that "immigrant" identity is scrubbed strategically from the episode's narrative teaser: "But unlike other kids at school, they had to keep their dating secret, because their parents disapproved. Both of them, but especially Adnan, were under special pressure at home" ("The Breakup"). The leap to "immigrant" parameters that Kang notes above becomes "special pressure" here "unlike other kids at school." In fact, other kids at school, as documented by *Serial* itself, did experience something like this. The willingness to "go there" rhetorically in the podcast and simultaneously spin and obfuscate it in the introduction in order to euphemize it betrays the anxiety and/or inability to contend responsibly with the racial dimensions of this narrative.

Koenig, furthermore, states in the first episode:

> And on paper, the case was like a Shakespearean mashup—young lovers from different worlds thwarting their families, secret assignations, jealousy, suspicion, and honor besmirched, the villain not a Moor exactly, but a Muslim all the same, and a final act of murderous revenge.

> ("The Alibi")

The passage begs not only *Othello* but also a racialized two-houses *Romeo and Juliet* in this quick hyperbolizing invocation of Shakespeare. The passage is so tightly stylized that it has blinded itself to the implications of what it is saying. Alemán writes: "an emerging body of literature utilizes the tenets of critical race theory as a lens from which to analyze traditional media content to locate majoritarian discourses about communities of color" (290). Koenig adopts the majoritarian discourse here, invoking in the name of the spectacle that racism, or at least the trace of that racism, implicit in Shakespeare's Moor. Then, immediately, the passage makes a value-laden decision that "Muslim" identity replaces (or trumps) and erases racial identity: not a racial identity (which like the designation "Moor" is something from the past), but instead a religious designation. The passage is rife with morally vexed aesthetic decisions that glare in the light of the kind of racially vested narrative analysis that critical race theory allows for. Koenig builds an entire podcast season that exculpates Adnan yet names him the villain here, invoking the (Muslim) honor besmirched cited in the prosecutor's case, which is lamented in the first two episodes. Koenig even flippantly invokes the idea that it is a revenge murder. Is this a red herring? Is this done in order to front the counterargument? Neither answered in the affirmative would mitigate the means. This reads more like the *Serial* team had no "voice of color." The voice of color thesis

> holds that because of their different histories and experiences with oppression, black, Indian, Asian, and Latino/a writers and thinkers may be able to communicate to their white counterparts matters that the whites are unlikely to know. Minority status, in other words, brings with it a presumed competence to speak about race and racism.

> (Delgado 10)

The failings of *Serial* that are so glaringly obvious to critics of color exist precisely because Koenig and her team worked from a white majoritarian privilege.

This criticism doesn't seek to fault the impulse or the efforts of the *Serial* team, but, beyond even what's been laid out so far, there is the voice-of-color thesis to contend with. Beyerstein's article in *The Observer* leads ironically with a prominent compilation of the photos of the leading figures on the team responsible for putting the podcast together: Koenig, Snyder, Chivvis, Condon, and Glass. For some, it is perhaps an unremarkable image. For people of color, it is immediately and viscerally striking. Koenig says of the detectives that investigated Adnan that they were well respected and known to do good work. Koenig and her team are clearly well respected and have done potentially genre-changing work, not to mention the impact the podcast is having locally on Syed's case and the legal system, and potentially on a larger scale as well. *Serial* fails, however, at erasing racial discourse all but completely from the season. Beyerstein's article carries the subtitle "Charges of 'Problematic' Racism Won't Stick to the Greatest Podcast Ever." The decision to include these photos, then, is ironic as it underscores, at a glance, how none of the main figures behind the podcast is a person of color. Just as Koenig asks why the detectives didn't check to see if there was a phone booth or follow up on the cell towers or the route that had to be driven, one must in all ethical responsibility ask why the *Serial* team didn't think it was necessary, prudent, ethical, liberal, advisable even, to call on the expertise of journalists and producers of color when developing a story this important, located in Baltimore, at Woodlawn High School, involving a cast of characters from a range of racial backgrounds, most of which weren't white. Those photographs and the scare-quoting of the word "problematic" in the subtitle is a sensational example of how to bury an ignored reality of the subtle and privileged racism for which *Serial* stands accused and of a reaffirmation of the majoritarian discourse. It doesn't take very sophisticated narrative analysis to unpack this, it should be noted, in order to clarify how bluntly problematic that racially majoritarian discourse is. While it may not be terribly surprising, for example, that there is very little written about racial discourse and the genre of true crime, it is more surprising when "allied" liberal podcasts, producers, and journalists refuse to consider a counterstory when it's a racial counterstory, fail to speak for ignored realities (when it's a racial reality), and neglect to analyze narrative (when it is a racial narrative). Critical race theory, in not flinching from the criticism of the Civil Rights Acts, in confirming that racism will never end, opens rhetorical space to level these accusations against *Serial* and Beyerstein's revealingly situated article.

While Durrani noted above that *Serial* speaks to the ignored reality of the Muslim community in a relatively complex manner, the podcast fails to take up the interconnected dimension of race. In fact, it actively works to erase this dimension. Koenig states, "Adnan claims he just wasn't that religious.

He was going to clubs and having sex with girls, and smoking weed from the time he was fourteen or fifteen. Culturally, yes a Muslim, but the rest, he says, not so much" ("The Breakup"). The rhetorical move borrows from the common bifurcation of Jewish identity as culturally or religiously Jewish. "The rest" conflates every other possible interconnected aspect of his Muslim identity into the container of religious belief. The rhetorical effect of disrupting the prosecutor's case for motive is clear and convincing, however, at a cost not only of ignoring the racial reality of the Muslim community but also of actively contributing to its erasure.

Koenig looks to Hae Min's diary for a kind of witness testimony as to Adnan's religious beliefs. Koenig qualifies this evidence, stating: "So, yeah, anytime someone is writing stuff down like 'sin' and 'devil' and 'religion means life' in reference to their secret relationship, that's not good. But ask the Muslim in question about it" ("The Breakup"). It is strange that, at this precise moment, Koenig's narrative analytical acumen and counter-storytelling diction breaks down again, reverting to an easy majoritarian perspective. Koenig in this episode rebuts the idea that Adnan is a practicing Muslim, given his womanizing teenage behavior. It is an effective argument. In this quotation, however, she briefly relies on the evidence that she's already impugned (the diary of a teenager) to resort to a qualifying instance, an echo really, of the kind of bigoted reduction of Muslim belief so pervasive in American discourse. This is followed immediately by a reference to Adnan as "the Muslim in question." The style, with blinders on, reads as breezy, whimsical, and lightening. It is an aesthetic move, nevertheless, that ignores the discursive racial power invoked by reducing Adnan, even if for that second and for those ends, to "the Muslim in question."

Finally, in the podcast, Jay's flat characterization contrasts suspiciously with Adnan's relatively more complex characterization. Jay is cast largely as "shady" in Episode 8. When Koenig does attend to the question of whether or not his "thuggish vibe was just a pose," she employs a story about Jay playfully, "goofily," trying to stab a friend. In any case, Koenig never unpacks the racial valence of such characterization and specific diction. Indeed, in both Jay's and Adnan's cases, the ways in which their characters flatten out has everything to do with racial tropes.

Jay's testimony and interviews contrast notably with Adnan's elocution. In the second interview with the police, Jay repeatedly says "uh" and "um" and curses, saying "bitch" and "fuck." His speaking style is notably more informal; Adnan does not curse, does not hedge with "um," and is more articulate. Koenig does not parse the difference in the formality/informality in their speech; does not discuss how race is a factor in how their elocution and pronunciation patterns will subtly influence the audience's sociohistorically informed assumptions (Jay as black and Adnan as not black); does not question when interviewees in Episode 8 use language such as "shady" and "thuggish" but instead passes on those racial tropes to the audience. The incisive narrative analysis that characterizes the rest of the podcast breaks down. Instead, the AAVE (African American Vernacular English) patterns are parked alongside the development of Jay-as-"shady." At odds with *Serial*'s modus operandi, this is therefore all the more glaringly evidence of not only its failings to engage in critical narrative analysis when it comes to race, nor merely its perpetuation of ignored realities, but its active participation in racially majoritarian discourse.

Does *Serial* cross an ethical line for aestheticizing true crime? When seen through the lens of critical race theory, no. *Serial* seeks to tell a counterstory to rebut the legal narrative about Adnan. In order to tell that story effectively, it draws on a number of aesthetic techniques—humanizing Adnan through characterization, for example—but actually downplays plot in the name of a more logical, problem-solving organization. Therefore, the cliffhanger plots, the suspense and spectacle, and the definitive endings that characterize the kind of true-crime narratives that are ethically suspect have no role here. The more "spectacular" of aesthetic techniques that are used are not the ends but the means to mobilizing the counterstory, speaking of ignored realities, and revealing the power relationships and issues in the narrative through thorough narrative analysis. Nevertheless, ironically, that professional storytelling technique, that aestheticization of the narrative, mobilized very much in the spirit of critical race theory, is repeatedly behind the racial erasure, the reification of ignored racial realities, and the invocation of majoritarian racial discourse despite the clear interest in counter-storytelling on other fronts.

Works Cited

Alemán, Sonya M. and Enrique Alemán. "Critical Race Media Projects Counterstories and Praxis (Re)Claim Chicana/o Experiences." *Urban Education* 51.3 (2016): 287–314. uex.sagepub.com. Web. 7 May 2016.

"The Alibi." *Serial*. Episode 1. 13 Oct. 2014. This American Life. Web.

Bell, Derrick A., Richard Delgado and Jean Stefancic. *The Derrick Bell Reader*. New York University Press, 2005. Print.

Beyerstein, Lindsay. "Not Problematic: In Defense of '*Serial*'." *Observer*. 18 Nov. 2014. Web. 8 May 2016.

"The Breakup." *Serial*. Episode 2. 13 Oct. 2014. This American Life. Web.

Browder, Laura. "True Crime." In *The Cambridge Companion to American Crime Fiction*. Ed. Catherine Ross Nickerson. Cambridge University Press, 2010. 121–134.

Delgado, Richard and Jean Stefancic. *Critical Race Theory: An Introduction*, 2nd ed. New York University Press, 2012. Print.

Dockterman, Eliana. "How *The Jinx* and *Serial* Strain the Blurry Ethical Lines of Crime Reporting." *Time.Com* (2015): N.PAG. *MAS Ultra—School Edition*. Web. 16 Apr. 2016.

Durrani, Mariam, Kevin Gotkin and Corrina Laughlin. "*Serial*, Seriality, and the Possibilities for the Podcast Format: Visual Anthropology." *American Anthropologist* 117.3 (2015): 1–4. *CrossRef*. Web. 7 May 2016.

Flanagin, Jake. "How 'True Crime' Went from Guilty Pleasure to High Culture." *Quartz*. 5 Jan. 2016. Web. 7 May 2016.

Gambini, Bert. "'*Serial*'s' Koenig Says Her Podcast Succeeds Because It's Real." *UB Reporter*. 12 Apr. 2016. Web. 16 Apr. 2016.

Haglund, David, Katy Waldman and Mike Pesca. "Was There an Ending? We Discuss the Final Episode of *Serial*." *Slate*. 18 Dec. 2014. Web. 7 May 2016.

Kang, Jay Caspian. "White Reporter Privilege." *The Awl*. Web. 7 May 2016.

Levin, Josh. "*Serial* Wasn't a Satisfying Story. It Was a Master Class in Investigative Journalism." *Slate*. 18 Dec. 2014. Web. 7 May 2016.

Lorde, Audre. "The Uses of Erotic: The Erotic as Power." In *The Black Feminist Cultural Criticism*. Ed. Jacqueline Bobo. Malden: Blackwell Publishers, 2001. 285–291.

Maerz, Melissa. "*Serial*: The Podcast You Need To Hear." *Entertainment Weekly* 1339 (2014): 14. *MasterFILE Premier*. Web. 14 Mar. 2016.

Wallace-Wells, Benjamin. "The Strange Intimacy of '*Serial*'." *Vulture*. 24 Nov. 2014. Web. 7 May 2016.

Contributors

Jillian DeMair teaches German language and literature at the University of Central Arkansas, where she has been Visiting Assistant Professor since fall 2015. Her research focuses on texts that self-consciously explore the limits of believability and authentic representation in their portrayals of crime and detection, implausible occurrences, and disruptions to the natural environment. She received her Ph.D. from Harvard University in 2013 with a dissertation titled "Telling about the Truth: Negotiations of Credibility in German Narratives."

Ryan Engley is a Ph.D. Candidate in English at the University of Rhode Island. His academic work has appeared in *The International Journal of Žižek Studies*, *Cinematic Cuts: Theorizing Film Endings*, and *The Ocean State Review*.

Erica Haugtvedt is currently a Senior Lecturer in English at Ohio State University. Her Ph.D., from Ohio State University, is in nineteenth-century British literature. Her research focuses on the Victorian serial novel and its contemporary remediations. Drawing upon narrative theory, media studies, and the history of the novel, Haugtvedt explores the reception of serial characters in the nineteenth century as antecedents to fandom and transmedia storytelling in the twentieth and twenty-first centuries.

Sandra Kumamoto Stanley is a Professor of American Literature at California State University, Northridge. She is the author of *Louis Zukofsky and the Transformation of a Modern American Poetics* and editor of *Other Sisterhoods: Literary Theory and U.S. Women of Color*. She has published in such journals as *Twentieth Century Literature*, *Critique*, *Journal of Modern Literature*, *MELUS*, and *Amerasia Journal*.

David Letzler is an independent scholar and the author of *The Cruft of Fiction: Mega-Novels and the Science of Paying Attention*, forthcoming in summer 2017. He lives in Queens, New York.

Ellen McCracken is a Professor in the Department of Spanish and Portuguese at the University of California, Santa Barbara. She is the author of *Decoding Women's Magazines: From* Mademoiselle *to* Ms., *New Latina Narrative: The Feminine Space of Postmodern Ethnicity, The Life and Writing of Fray Angélico Chávez* (winner of a Southwest Book Award), and *Paratexts and Performance in the Novels of Junot Díaz and Sandra Cisneros.*

Charli Valdez, recipient of a Fulbright for his dissertation research in Spain, received his A.M. in Comparative Literature at Brown University and his Ph.D. in Literature and Creative Writing at the University of Houston. He has published fiction and scholarship in the *Saranac Review, Film and Literary Modernism*, and *The Great Recession in Fiction, Film, and Television: Twenty-First-Century Bust Culture.* He is from Albuquerque, New Mexico.

Index

Printed in the United States
by Baker & Taylor Publisher Services